The Golden Threa

The Golden Thread of God's Love

From South Africa to the UK and Beyond

A narrative of an 'ordinary' man with
an extraordinary God

Gill Ganie

YouCaxton Publications
Oxford & Shrewsbury

ISBN 978-1-913425-18-0
Published by YouCaxton Publications 2020
YCBN: 01

YouCaxton Publications

enquiries@youcaxton.co.uk

Contents

Introduction

On the face of it, Omar appeared to be a relatively ordinary man. Within minutes of meeting him, most people formed some sort of opinion because he would either offend them or charm them! Being beautifully open could sometimes have detrimental consequences: he would dive straight in with, 'So what do you feel called to do? What's your life goal?' Some would respond to these challenging words, others were left flummoxed and wondered why they had been put on the spot in that way. Either way, it certainly got them thinking.

***

Omar was the funniest man that Gill, his wife, had ever met. Funny in a sweet, naïve way. And loudly extravagant in every way – with his resources, his love, his thoughts and his feelings. He would happily declare his undying love for his wife publicly, in his unique, expressive way. He could also disagree loudly in public, much to Gill's embarrassment. Quietly, she would try to say, 'Don't worry we'll discuss it later', to which often came the reply, 'No, we need to sort it out now. What's the problem? No-one's listening.'

Gill knew only too well by the surrounding hush of listeners that many were intrigued to hear the outcome of this conflicting dialogue.

Prologue

Omar sounded overwhelmed, excited, a little confused when he rang his wife, Gill, from work. She was busy at her workplace and wondered what the urgency was. However, knowing her husband well, there was often a story to tell, some exciting news to relay or suchlike and today was no different – although slightly more mind-blowing…

Chapter 1

Unusual Beginnings

"I am the Alpha and the Omega," says the Lord God, "who is, and who was, and who is to come, the Almighty." Revelation 1:8

Omar Ganie was born on the 24th May 1958 but his birth was registered on the 20th July 1960. Why the two-year gap? he always wondered. He was extremely proud of this unusual birth certificate, which revealed that he was born in South Africa but registered in the UK two years later. He took delight in presenting it to interested observers, who were generally intrigued by this rare phenomenon.

Omar's mother, Radha, was a Hindu and a South African of Asian descent; she had been born in 1926 in Pietermaritzburg within the high-caste Naidoo family, who were very wealthy. She had nine siblings and they owned at least three or four houses. Her father ran a real estate business and Radha would do his bookkeeping. She took pride in serving her father and, among other tasks, would meticulously clean his smoking pipes and prepare his clothes ready for work. She was a faithful, reliable and respectful young daughter growing up in apartheid South Africa.

Regarding his birth in South Africa, Omar had always been told by his mother that she had moved away and settled in the UK, where she met and married his father Abdool (known as Ray) Ganie, a Muslim man. She told Omar that his grandfather was very angry that she had married a Muslim. Ray had been a pen friend and Radha said she had run away from her home in South Africa to

England because she had fallen in love with him. Ray had been born in what was then known as British Guyana in the capital, George Town, in 1927 and had moved to England in 1954. He was one of ten children.

Ray had not been a practising Muslim when they married as it would have been very unusual for a committed Muslim to marry a Hindu. He was very charming and evidently swept Radha off her feet. Soon she was expecting his child and it was at this time that she received news that her father was seriously ill. She therefore travelled by ship back to South Africa to visit him.

Apparently, during the visit Radha's father became extremely angry when he discovered that she was pregnant and had married outside of her culture and religion. He intimated that the baby would be placed in an orphanage, of which he was one of the founders, and thereafter he or she would be put up for adoption. So a plan was hatched and quickly put into effect: Radha was taken by two of her brothers to Cape Town by car. There, the baby would be born secretly and then looked after, for a short period, by a Muslim friend of the family, Uncle Tassim, and his wife – thereby escaping the orphanage and possible adoption.

This proved to be the beginning of the golden thread of God's love – a love that saved, protected, shielded, and defended Omar at all costs. The story went that soon after Omar was born, he was taken with his mother by ship back to England. As for the two-year gap between his birth and registration – Omar's mother said that his father did not get around to it until about two years later! Although these circumstances were unusual, Omar always believed this account of his birth to be true; he had no reason to doubt it.

Chapter 2

Mighty to Save

'He lifted me out of the slimy pit, out of the mud and mire; he set my feet on a rock and gave me a firm place to stand.' Psalm 40:2

Omar's earliest childhood memories were of living in a big house in Highbury, near Stoke Newington in North London with his parents and little sister Anusuya (Ana), younger by two years. Two other families also lived in the house. When Ana was born, Omar was sent to stay with his uncle for a couple of weeks while his mum recovered and adjusted to having a new baby.

The family lived on the top floor of the house and although space was limited, they were happy there. Omar attended the local school, Princess May Primary, and life seemed to be going pretty well. That is, until a neighbour was stabbed nearby, which prompted Omar's mother to hunt for a safer area to raise their children. Thus, when Omar was seven years old, he and the family uprooted and moved away from the environment where they had been so settled prior to the fatal event. His dad in particular had loved living in North London surrounded by close friends and some of his brothers, with whom he had regularly played card games or dominoes.

Omar and Ana both had fond memories of those early days; Ana still remembers often being carried on her father's shoulders, feeling very safe and loved. They had both basked in the joyous security of their family life.

The move was to Sutton, a leafy suburb in South West London, vastly different from Highbury. They were, in fact, the only Indian family in the area for a number of years.

Omar was very aware of being 'different' but his vivacious character soon won him many friends. His sister Ana recalls how he always looked out for her, not letting anyone mistreat her and get away with it – he took his 'big brother' role very seriously. Omar also concerned himself with Ana's welfare at home, which was no longer the happy place it had been in North London.

Since moving, their father had become very resentful, often exhibiting his anger directly at the children or their mother. It was a fearful existence although, according to Ana, Omar seemed fearless. He usually found an escape route when necessary, such as the time his dad was angry with him about a particular incident. Omar ran out through the back of the house and jumped over the fence to seek temporary refuge.

In spite of some of the negative impacts of the move to Sutton, it soon became clear that this was part of God's plan and the beginning of miraculous salvation in this family. When Omar was eight years old, God's golden thread continued to weave in his life through an elderly neighbour, Mrs Thumbwood. Mrs Thumbwood loved Jesus and was probably the first Christian that Omar had met; she gave him a bible and also took him and Ana to Sunday school. This was the beginning of Omar's adventure with Jesus. He would take his bible to school and when not playing football would often read it in the playground. He particularly enjoyed reading the book of Romans in the New Testament. Omar loved school; he felt safe there. Outside of school he joined the Boys' Brigade and wore his uniform with pride. This organisation was another way through which he learned more about God's love for him.

When Omar was eleven years old, he attended Cheam High School. As he was an outgoing and friendly boy, it was quite disconcerting for him when travelling to school by bus that the seat next to him always remained empty until there was no other space available. He could only surmise that this was due to the fact that he was the only non-white person on the bus. It was a joy to him one day when at the age of thirteen, another boy, who he had not met before, boarded the bus and sat beside him. They got chatting and this was to become the beginning of a lifelong friendship between Omar and Roy. They were very different in character but both had a positive impact on each other – Roy and his family helped to bring some stability into Omar's life and Omar proved to be a reliable friend to Roy. As Roy would sometimes miss school due to ill health, Omar would try to help him catch up with his schoolwork.

In many ways, Omar and Roy were inseparable and even though they were in different classes, they always arranged to meet on the bus when travelling to and from school. Most days, Omar would spend time at Roy's house after school – and he would also turn up there when Roy had not been at school. It was another safe haven for Omar, a peaceful refuge vastly different from his own home environment. Many happy hours were spent playing chess, backgammon, dominoes or kicking a plastic football in the hallway – Roy's mother must have been delighted!

Omar was a boy who would usually bound around with lots of energy; he had an open personality and in many ways was quite vulnerable and naïve. Roy relays the story of when he, another friend and Omar went swimming. Knowing that Omar couldn't swim (Omar was also keenly aware of this), they suggested that Omar should jump into the deep end. He promptly did this and almost drowned. Thankfully, Roy managed to rescue him – dragging him, coughing and spluttering, to the side of the pool. That was the last time Omar went anywhere near deep water unless he was on a very safe boat!

There was just one Ganie family holiday, which took place when Omar was fourteen years old. He, his mother and sister enjoyed a week in Spain, which was a very special time. Another memorable holiday Omar had as a teenager was at the age of sixteen when he went to Portland, near Weymouth, with Roy and his family. This family holiday was a unique experience for Omar and he appreciated being included in Roy's family in this way.

During Omar's sixteenth year there was particular period of searching for a tangible relationship with God. During this time, he attended church more frequently and suddenly everything he had learnt about Jesus seemed to make sense. He was totally awakened to the reality that Jesus was real and loved Omar just the way he was; Jesus had died for him so that his sins could be forgiven, and Omar had the promise of eternal life.

'For God so loved the world that he gave his one and only Son, that whoever believes in him shall not perish but have eternal life.' John 3:16.

Omar hungrily accepted God's word (the Bible), read it, believed it and trusted it to be true. His life was transformed. He was saved from the miry pit!

As Omar increasingly began to relate to Jesus, it would be an understatement to say that he regularly shared his views with those close to him, particularly his mum and sister. He knew it was a life-and-death situation and they needed to be saved so that they, too, could spend eternity with Jesus.

Omar also tried to impose his beliefs on Roy. He was a passionate evangelist and was especially adamant that those who were important to him should have every opportunity for the eternal life with which he knew he was blessed. Roy, though, was having none of it and told Omar so in no uncertain terms. Omar continued to pray, totally believing

God would answer his prayers and bring Roy to faith in Him.

The local Baptist church Omar attended was very supportive to him in his early days as a believer. He also persuaded his sister Ana to attend, although she preferred the church youth club. While Omar staunchly tried to evangelise Ana, she never felt that he judged her lifestyle and knew that he was very accepting of her. She realised how seriously Omar took his faith, especially when he announced that he was giving away all of his secular music, including Alvin Stardust! This, in her eyes, was crazy.

Ana did have an awareness of God's presence at times though: on one particular occasion, she remembers walking down the stairway at school when she suddenly felt the presence of God envelop her. She felt His amazing peace and could only conclude that her brother's prayers were being answered.

Chapter 3

Elohim: King of Kings, Lord of Lords

'Trust in the Lord with all your heart and lean not on your own understanding.' Proverbs 3:5

With his mother's encouragement, Omar aspired to study medicine. This would mean concentrated study and the attainment of exemplary grades. He achieved five 'O' levels but failed Biology and Physics, which were required for medicine. His best results were in English Literature and Religious Knowledge, followed closely by Chemistry. As the situation at home between Omar and his father was becoming untenable, it was agreed that the best option would be for Omar to study for his 'A' level exams at boarding school.

In fact, for the majority of Omar's adult life, he and his father were not in contact. This was predominantly due to his father's violent temper, which frequently flared up without reasonable cause. Later in life, however, there were a few years when they renewed their relationship and Omar treasured this reunion; although, sadly, it did not last.

Therefore, in September 1974, this hopeful sixteen-year-old left London to arrive as a boarder at Merchant Taylors' School in Crosby, Liverpool. As he entered the main school gate the sight of this large, redbrick 19th Century school must have appeared pretty daunting to him. The school was founded in 1620 by John Harrison, a citizen and Merchant Taylor of London, who was born in Great Crosby.

Omar settled as a boarder and was given responsibilities as school prefect. School reports stated that he was considerate, polite and prepared to work hard. He was also described as cheerful and responsible, although sometimes lacking in self-confidence.

Financially, times were very hard for the Ganie family during this period – school fees were high and it was a huge sacrifice for the family to send Omar to this prestigious school. Omar was not able to go home at the weekends like many of the other boarders. He managed as best he could with few resources. His sister Ana recalls Omar informing her that he attached a piece of cheese to some string and hung it out of the window to keep it fresh… there was clearly some logic in this!

Academically, Omar was disappointed not to achieve the grades he needed, so he decided to repeat them at Davies College in London. Although his aim was to study medicine, he was aware that a positive alternative would be to study Chemistry at university; he particularly enjoyed and achieved good grades in this subject.

Living back at home, the year of 1976 was very significant in Omar's Christian walk. He joined a Charismatic church (Charismatic Christianity, also known as Spirit-Filled Christianity, is a form of Christianity that emphasises the work of the Holy Spirit, spiritual gifts, and modern-day miracles as an everyday part of a believer's life) and was baptised in a local river, confessing his faith and allegiance to Jesus very publicly.

It was a very hot and dry summer, and rain was desperately needed. Omar often recounted that whilst travelling home from the baptism there was a sudden torrential downpour, which he believed was God-sent. Following the baptism, his mother refused to speak to him for two weeks and frequently stated adamantly, 'I was born a Hindu, I will die a Hindu!' Undeterred, Omar continued to press on in prayer for her salvation.

Omar did not achieve the required grades to study medicine but did attain a grade 'A' in Chemistry. He therefore decided to undertake a degree in Chemistry with a view to teaching. He was pleased to discover later that he had a natural teaching gift – God's golden thread continued! Since Omar applied late for a university place, he went through Clearing (which is how universities and colleges fill any places they still have on their courses). He was offered a place at Manchester University and thus set off on his next adventure.

Omar was initially accommodated in Moberly Towers with overseas students – which he found to be a great place for evangelism. In addition to his evangelistic efforts and academic studies, Omar attended and became very involved in the local church. He enjoyed working with the youth and playing in the church football team (where his team-mates called him 'Stick' due to his very slight build) among other activities. The church Omar attended provided excellent care of students and many families were allocated a student to look out for and mentor. Consequently, a firm, lifelong friendship developed between Omar and Ian and Sheila Davies.

Ian became one of many father figures in Omar's life, and Omar had great respect and love for him. Ian was on hand to assist him out of numerous scrapes, such as the time when Omar thought he had locked himself out of his lodgings late one very wet night. He rang Ian, who promptly drove the thirty-minute journey to meet him. When Ian arrived, Omar was nowhere to be seen, so a concerned Ian drove the streets in pursuit of him – but to no avail. He eventually gave up, hoping and praying that Omar was safe. He later discovered that Omar had found his keys in his pocket after all, so had let himself in and gone straight to bed. Sweet!

Chapter 4

A Steep Learning Curve

'If you declare with your mouth, "Jesus is Lord," and believe in your heart that God raised him from the dead, you will be saved.' Romans 10:9

Having finished his Chemistry degree in 1980 and completing a Certificate in Education in 1981, Omar was employed as a science teacher in Stratford Secondary School, in Stratford, London. Here, he was able to develop his teaching gift. His sense of fun and frequent good-humoured teasing generally went down well; although there were times when he inadvertently overstepped the mark.

Being quite a perfectionist and always keen to do the very best with what was put before him, Omar worked long, hard hours at school. Initially, at the young age of twenty-three years, he was not much older in age or maturity than some of his pupils. He had to learn to maintain a professional distance and not be too familiar with them or, as he soon discovered, this could prove to be hazardous!

His first teaching post in East London was a steep learning curve and Omar had to become streetwise, quickly. He was assaulted twice by previous school pupils, which terrified him and alerted him to being extremely aware of his safety. He sold his beloved Hi-Fi music system to a friend so that he could purchase a bike, which made travelling to and from school safer. These years were challenging but, thanks to the support of good friends from his local church and the knowledge that God was with him, he got through.

Much to his disappointment, Omar's mum and sister had yet to become Christians. After much pestering they agreed to come and stay with him, knowing that he planned to invite some friends to pray for them. Ana agreed just to appease him, as she knew how important it was to him. So there they were, chairs placed in the middle of the room; Omar and several other Christians gathered around them praying. His mother and Ana, without real understanding, but because they wanted to keep Omar happy, repeated some words of repentance and asked Jesus into their lives. They were then told that they were Christians!

Omar, in his usual determined way, was doing all he could to get them into God's kingdom. He took them to his church the next day and also explained to them the importance of finding a suitable church to attend close to their home in Sutton. They duly obeyed and to Omar's delight, thankfully, within the next few weeks had voluntarily responded to God's call on their lives and went forward in response to an 'altar call' during the church service. (An altar call is a tradition in some evangelical Christian churches in which those who wish to make a new spiritual commitment to Jesus Christ are invited to come forward publicly.) They willingly gave their lives to Jesus – oh, what great rejoicing in Heaven that day!

With regards to Omar's parents' relationship – after years of living disconnected lives they finally separated during the early 1980's, subsequently to divorce in 1982. Following the divorce, Omar's father Ray renewed his Muslim beliefs and attended his local Mosque regularly; this also gave him a social network, which helped him with his loneliness. He moved back to his beloved North London from Sutton in the years following the divorce.

Chapter 5

Young Love

'A threefold cord is not easily broken.' Ecclesiastes 4:12

Omar was a great planner and always loved to think ahead. He had visions and dreams, and was the sort of person to write his requests before the Lord. He would present them, pray over them and believe that God would provide the answer. As a Bible-believing Christian he would, with God's help, always try to live his life according to biblical principles, including petitioning to God.

Philippians 4:6-7 Do not be anxious about anything, but in every situation, by prayer and petition, with thanksgiving, present your requests to God. And the peace of God, which transcends all understanding, will guard your hearts and your minds in Christ Jesus.

1 John 5:14-15 This is the confidence we have in approaching God: that if we ask anything according to his will, he hears us. And if we know that he hears us — whatever we ask — we know that we have what we asked of him.

Omar applied his usual approach in the case of his search for a wife. He had been praying for a wife a few years earlier and God had told him* that she was not yet a Christian. Omar had done his best to be as patient as possible but this was not his greatest asset. 'That's it,' said Omar to his friend and mentor Ian Davies in December 1983, 'I've waited long enough now. If God doesn't give me a wife in the next two weeks I'm just going to go and find one!' Ian tried to tell Omar that it doesn't work quite like that but Omar was unperturbed; he had made up his mind. The search, however, was put on hold as Omar was suddenly struck down with a serious bout of flu. He spent the whole of the Christmas period unwell, alone and crying out to God for his future, whilst trusting that God that would find him a wife at the right time.

January came and with it an unexpected invitation to lunch. The invitation came from Omar's friend, Jackie, who was visiting her friend Alison for the weekend. Alison was studying to become an Occupational Therapist and was on a short placement in Hackney, London. She attended Hampden Chapel, where she had become good friends with a young woman called Gill. A unique lunch was arranged for these four young Christians, who met after church in January 1984 in Hackney Hospital nurses' home. They had a fun afternoon together chatting, praying and singing. Omar and Gill washed the dishes, and the beginnings of a close bond commenced from that moment. He used her name a lot; she liked that. He had a mass of black, curly hair, was kind of cute in a lanky way – and very skinny, it has to be said. Gill was oblivious of the oncoming tidal wave of love and romance that was about to hit her!

The following month, Omar invited Gill and Alison for lunch at his rented flat in Stratford, London, with some other friends, and impressed them by cooking a roast dinner. After lunch Omar took his friends to see a flat that he was planning to buy, explaining that, due to the high mortgage, he would be unable to tithe. (To give tithes is a biblical principle of giving the first tenth of one's income to the work of the church; it is voluntary but many Christians believe it is an important principle.) Shock, horror: Gill's instant reaction was that he couldn't possibly go ahead then; it would be out of the question! Such boldness – where did that come from? Nothing else was said on the subject and later Omar took them to his church where, by chance, that evening, he was preaching.

When Gill got back to the nurses' home at The Mothers' Hospital in Hackney, where she resided as a student midwife, her friend Carol popped into her room to say 'hi'. 'What's he like then, this Omar?' she asked with a knowing smile on her face, as though she felt there may be a special relationship brewing between this young man and Gill. That was the first inkling Gill had that something might be transpiring in her life. 'Um, he's nice, very open, transparent – not like anyone I've met before.' The only other vague indication Gill had that some sort of change was coming – although she was clueless as to what it was about – was that during that particular winter she had felt an inexplicable excitement about the coming summer and had commented as such to Carol.

Meanwhile, when Omar was alone that evening, contemplating the day's events, he felt God say to him, 'What do you think about Gill?'* He smiled and his thoughts were, 'I want to marry that girl!' He could not get over what she had said about tithing: very forward, he thought… and very spiritual!

Omar wanted to be with someone sold out for Jesus, someone willing to challenge him, love him – and be encouraged and challenged by him, too. He did not waste much time before he rang Gill to invite her out for a meal. He almost declared his undying love there and then in that call, which was taken by Gill on the only available communal phone based in the corridor of her accommodation; there were no mobile phones in those days. Gill was about to go on to night duty and informed Omar that she would pray about it and let him know. Since becoming a Christian, Gill had decided that she did not want to date anyone unless she was sure that this was very possibly going to lead to a serious commitment and that he was likely to be 'the one'. She was very aware that this was a major decision and was not going to take it lightly. Omar agreed to call again. Soon.

After much prayer and deliberation, a first date was set: 10th March, 1984. They met at Bethnal Green tube station and travelled to the recommended 'Red Fort' Indian restaurant in Dean Street, Soho. Omar got there first, of course; he was very keen. There he was, waiting on the corner with a beautiful bunch of flowers for Gill. Gill's first thought was, 'Sweet, but oh my gosh I have to carry these all around London!' It was a lovely evening. There was a special connection between them and they chatted freely, learning many things about each other's lives. It felt completely natural to hold hands on the way home. They prayed together before going their separate ways, and arranged to meet within the next few days.

Over the next couple of weeks, they met a number of each other's friends and spoke to one another daily on the phone; in fact, whenever Gill got back from her shift, she would be informed by one of the other students, 'He's been calling for you.' Omar had found his wife and was not going to let anything stand in his way. They spent many hours, day and night, on that phone; it was a wonder that Gill didn't receive complaints for blocking the only phone line!

So, two weeks after their first date, Omar proposed. Gill was ready to propose to him if he had not done so, so they were definitely on the same page. They were acutely aware that this may not be the usual course of events for most couples, many of whom spend considerable time dating, seeking wise counsel from friends, family and church leaders as appropriate.

Omar and Gill believed with all their hearts that God had brought them together at this point in their lives and were thankful to have the blessing of their families, friends and their church pastors. They frequently spent time praying together and their intention was always to keep Jesus central in their relationship. Omar often prayed using the scripture, 'A threefold cord is not easily broken' (Ecclesiastes 4:12, Geneva Bible). Amusingly, he was pleased that Gill liked cats – apparently that was important, as he had a very pregnant cat, which was about to produce several kittens. Omar passed the test question as to whether he thought capital punishment was right: 'No!' Phew – Gill would not have agreed to marry him if they had differed on that one. Omar wanted to ask Gill's father for her hand in marriage but she told him not to, as she thought it was old fashioned. Omar always felt bad about that. Plans went ahead for an August wedding. It was a busy five months but they believed that God had miraculously brought them together, so why wait?

Gill soon learnt even more that Omar loved Jesus with a passion, as she also did; that he was quite opinionated, usually right (in his view), hated queuing for *anything,* was quick to say what he thought (often thinking about it afterwards); and was wonderfully demonstrative and beautifully emotional. He was also not the most patient person she had met, but had such a love and extravagant enthusiasm for life that many of his faults could be overlooked. As she learned to love him more and more, it was easy to ignore his weaknesses and sometimes exasperating ways. No-one could be cross with this man for long. He made saying sorry an art form – not that he wasn't sincere; being the transparent person that he was, Gill knew she could trust him with her life.

On the 25th of August 1984, the wedding took place at Hampden Chapel in Hackney. Omar's best friend, Roy, was best man and was on hand to give advice and support to this very excited groom. A coach load of Gill's friends and family arrived from Bristol and Omar, with his usual audacious character, was on board the coach before anyone had a chance to disembark, introducing himself and shaking hands with the somewhat baffled guests. Omar's pastor, John Barr, officiated at the wedding and based his sermon on Psalm 37, which became a particularly significant scripture to Omar and Gill, especially verses 3-6.

'Trust in the Lord and do good; dwell in the land and enjoy safe pasture. Take delight in the Lord, and he will give you the desires of your heart. Commit your way to the Lord; trust in Him and He will do this: He will make your righteous reward shine like the dawn, your vindication like the noonday sun.'

Following the unique wedding celebration, Omar and Gill started to discover new things about each other daily, the first being the morning after the wedding when Omar was up and off out to find a Sunday Times, which apparently was imperative to have every Sunday, no matter where he was! On occasions when away from home, Omar would often drive miles in his quest to find his beloved Sunday Times. Then if he did not get chance to read it straight away, it would be put somewhere safe to ensure there was no chance of anyone else getting to it first. Gill often rummaged through the paper looking for the Style magazine, very conscious of being observed by a worried-looking Omar, whose main concern was that his paper did not get crumpled.

Gill quickly discovered that Omar was a very determined person and if he decided to do something, nothing or no-one would be able to stand in his way. If something needed fixing, either he resolved to get it fixed there and then himself, however inconvenient it might be, or he would find someone able to fix it. Likewise, Omar could be quite impulsive. If he decided that 'now' was a good time to start decorating a room, then 'now' it was. On would go painting gear, out came the buckets, paint, brushes, rollers – the lot. Gill soon learned that there was no point trying to argue, but she did have to quickly rush ahead to make the necessary preparations: put floor covering down and rub down paintwork before Omar appeared wielding a paintbrush in one hand and roller in the other. Usually a messy business!

Early in their marriage, during a visit to Gill's grandmother in Chew Stoke, near Bristol, Omar agreed to help by mowing the lawn. Being quite a novice at this, but keen as ever, he set about the task and was soon in full swing. However, he had not quite negotiated the boundaries or the fact that at the edge of the lawn there was a low hedge with a steep bank on the other side. Needless to say, Omar suddenly fell backwards through the hedge! Thankfully unscathed by the incident, he brushed himself down and continued with the job in hand.

Omar had many unique characteristics and comical ways – one being the way he would ask where a particular item could be found in a shop. He would approach a shop assistant and say, for example, 'B*ananas*'. That was it – one word – to which there was usually a look of puzzlement. This was strange for Omar, who was usually a man of many words. So, looking a bit bemused himself, he would repeat the word, usually a little louder, and the assistant would look at him as if they wondered if he was randomly starting a word association game and whether they should maybe reply, '*Apples!*' If Gill was there, Omar would look at her questioningly and she would interpret for him. He often said he felt like an alien in this world and, it seems, frequently behaved like one too. In fact, shopping or eating out with Omar could indeed be an embarrassing pastime, particularly when he often loudly exclaimed, 'WHAAT', when the bill was produced!

The book of Hebrews talks about people who lived by faith and admitted that they were aliens and strangers on earth: *'All these people were still living by faith when they died. They did not receive the things promised; they only saw them and welcomed them from a distance. And they admitted that they were aliens and strangers on earth.' (Hebrews 11:13.)*

** The relationship between Christians and Jesus is one that involves them walking closely with Him and seeking Him for guidance in their lives. When they pray, Christians often experience an impression or particular peace about certain situations.*
God has a plan for every one of us. Many people go through life without ever thinking about it, but that doesn't change the fact that God put us here for a purpose. We are not here by accident; we are here because God put us here. And He put us here for a reason — so we could come to know Him in a personal way and then live the way He wants us to live.
This is the greatest discovery you will ever make: you were created to know God and to be His friend forever. God not only has a general purpose for each of us, but He also has a specific plan for each of our lives. God knows all about you, and He has a plan for you.
That's why you can pray and seek God's will when you face decisions, and it is why you can know God is with you every moment of the day.
The Bible says, "Teach me your way, O Lord; lead me in a straight path." (Psalm 27:11). (Ref: God's Will by Billy Graham.)
The Bible says, "Trust in the Lord with all your heart and lean not on your own understanding; in all your ways acknowledge Him, and He will make your paths straight." (Proverbs 3:5-6)
When we commit to Christ, we should submit every decision we face to Him. When we sincerely want God's will above all else, He will help us know what is right.

Chapter 6

Blessed to be a Blessing

'He tends his flock like a shepherd: He gathers the lambs in his arms and carries them close to his heart; he gently leads those that have young.' Isaiah 40:11

Nine months after Omar and Gill were married came the arrival of their first baby, Timothy. Fifteen months later, along came Sarah and within four years of getting married, the final addition, Rachel. Busy times!

Prayer for the children began before they were born and continued following their arrival. Omar prophesied when Gill was expecting Timothy that he was indeed a boy – even though there were no sex-determining scans in those days – and would be called Timothy Daniel, a 'leader of people'. He prophesied that Sarah would be like a princess and before she was born, they believed that God impressed on them to name her 'Sarah', which they later discovered does in fact mean 'Princess'. Their third blessing, Rachel, also brought great joy and a close bond was quickly formed between her and Omar; she was very much a 'Daddy's girl'. At her dedication, the pastor John Barr prophesied that she would be used in healing (revealed later in her work as a physiotherapist where she would physically treat and also pray in her heart for healing for her clients) and that at some point she would leave these shores to serve God abroad.

Those early years were hectic and challenging in many ways – Omar was just learning how to be a husband, then rapidly needed to learn how to be a father too. Gill was super-hormonal and there were indeed some fiery clashes at times. With support from friends, mentors, their church leaders and, most of all, from Jesus they stayed the course and grew closer as a couple and as a family unit. Prayer always featured strongly in their lives and their hearts' desire was to raise their children in God's ways and for the children to choose to love Jesus for themselves.

Financially, the family very much needed to trust the Lord as on paper there was often not enough to cover the monthly expenses. This was especially the case when they moved from a flat to a house in 1988 and between finding the house and moving in, the interest rates rose so much that the mortgage was no longer affordable. God never let them down; He always met their needs. 'And my God will meet all your needs according to the riches of his glory in Christ Jesus' (Philippians 4:19). People would randomly arrive with bags of food; one particularly significant occasion was when a young man in his twenties appeared at a time when Gill had not been able to do the weekly food shop due to a lack of funds. He seemed embarrassed as he delivered two bags of groceries and said he felt God had directed him. This was indeed a Godsend!

During this time of apparent financial drought, Omar was unexpectedly promoted to Head of Science, due to staff sickness. This covered the excess bills! There were regular dances and jigs around the house when such answers to prayer came – such joy and thankfulness to their loving Heavenly Father.

***

Snapshots into family life

Family outings were numerous and great fun when the children were young, often to parks, the seaside and suchlike. On one occasion, when Rachel was about four years old, they were spending the day at Southend-on-Sea; they were walking along the promenade enjoying some chips for their lunch. They had planned to go into the amusement arcade and Rachel, in Omar's opinion, was taking far too long to finish her chips. Being his impetuous self, he took the cone of chips from her, told her to look up and open her mouth, tipped in the remaining chips and declared, 'There you go!' and headed off towards the amusement arcade, leaving Rachel looking somewhat bemused.

Requests were often taken quite literally. Once, during a holiday, their young daughters were in the sea on their giant-sized rubber ring. Gill asked Omar to keep an eye on them while she went to have a look around the little beach boutique. Upon arriving back to the beach, she asked where the girls were. Omar pointed at two dots on the horizon and casually said, 'There they are.' 'Aaaah, right,' was all Gill could think to utter before heading to the sea to bring them safely back to land!

Omar had a number of idiosyncrasies: one was to exhibit his infamous double-jointed fingers which, in all honesty, bent all the wrong ways. He often offered these weirdly shaped hands to his daughters as they walked together to the local shops whilst saying, 'I'm the beauty, you're the beast.' They never tired of his zany wit – or maybe they were just humouring him?

Rachel remembers when Omar used to put her to bed; he would put his head on her chest and sound out her heartbeat, 'badum badum!' He would then to tuck her in and read a story. He used to read the children's Bible, then later progressed onto the tweens' Bible, which was suitable between their childhood and teenage years. Rachel also recalls when Omar attended to watch her recite her poems at infant school. As she walked nervously towards the microphone, she was always encouraged to see Omar standing with his arms crossed, smiling and looking so proud.

Teaching each of his children to ride their bikes was a rewarding pastime for Omar. He would run with them, holding the saddle, and let go – sometimes when they were not aware that he was going to do so. Yet he always stayed close enough to pick them up when they became unbalanced and fell off. None of them gave up until they had mastered it – and Omar was one very proud Daddy!

When their son Tim was about ten years old, he was thrilled when his parents bought him a new bike for his birthday. He was out riding one day when two teenagers, a boy and a girl, managed to steal his bike. Distraught, Tim ran back home where he relayed to his parents what had happened. Omar stood at the bottom of the stairs and said, 'OK, we are going to pray, we have a big Daddy in Heaven.' He prayed that the bike would be returned. Gill then went out to look for it, praying for guidance as she went. She felt God lead her down a certain road and as she was walking past a group of girls, she heard one saying, 'I've nicked a bike, I've nicked a bike, I'm going cycling tomorrow!' Gill quickly ran home to get reinforcements, and returned with Omar and their three young children. When Omar approached the girl, Michelle, she initially denied all knowledge of the bicycle, but then gave an address in Hackney where they could find the bike. Gill took Tim with her to the address, which they found to be false. However, there then followed a series of miraculous events which led them to Michelle's front door! When they arrived there, Gill explained to Michelle's father that the girl had 'borrowed' the bike from Tim earlier and they now wanted it back. He was clearly very displeased with his daughter and promised that it would be returned the following morning. True to his word, he arrived at their home with the bike and a forlorn daughter in tow. Yes, they did have a big Daddy in Heaven and He cared for all their needs.

There were many other fun activities over the years, one being an annual cricket match that Omar arranged in the local park with people from church – great times! He usually bowled extra hard against his son Tim, showing no mercy. There were also one-on-one games of cricket with Tim, family cricket games and family football matches at various London parks. Victoria Park in Bethnal Green was a particular favourite.

In addition to playing, Omar absolutely loved to watch practically every sport. He would get totally engrossed, often raising the roof with his cheers and shouts when there was a football match, cricket match, tennis match, snooker or golf tournament…or basically any sport on TV at any time. If his team scored, won or was about to win, he would be up from his seat yelling at the TV, shouting 'yee-hah!' and giving high fives to anyone available. He was famous for his high fives and these usually accompanied most conversations; Omar had such amazing enthusiasm for life, which was surely God-given.

Above all else, the most important thing that his children learnt from him was to love Jesus with all their heart, to trust Him with their life and to bring everything before the Lord, who loves them and who answers their prayers.

Chapter 7

Growing Years

'But as for me and my household, we will serve the Lord.' Joshua 24:15

Omar and Gill's hearts' desire was to serve God abroad as missionaries and they prayed into this for many years. Knowing that he was born in South Africa, Omar was keen to visit his homeland, so in 1999 the whole family set off on this adventure, which was to have a massive impact on all of their lives.

The stark contrast of rich and poor is very evident in the beautiful city of Cape Town, South Africa. The backdrop to the entire city is the majestic Table Mountain, which is frequently clothed in clouds – locally referred to as 'The Tablecloth'. With the mountain to the right and the Atlantic Ocean to the left, the stunning setting can almost cause one to forget the devastating history and ongoing inequalities in this country. The indigenous population of Cape Town, mainly the Khoisan and mixed-race groups, have long struggled with identity issues, which they are working hard to address. A city full of complexities!

Whilst they were in Cape Town, in addition to lots of exciting sightseeing, the Ganie family attended a Christian conference and met an amazing South African couple, Siviwe and Desmeline. Siviwe arranged to take them to Gugulethu, one of the townships. They were struck and saddened to see such poverty in this country – which in many other ways is so prosperous.

Upon their return to the UK it was clear to both Omar and Gill that this is where God wanted them to serve Him.

If it wasn't for Gill's resistance, Omar would probably have packed his bags and been on the next flight, but with careful thought and prayer he realised that this needed some long-term planning. Life, therefore, continued much as usual, whilst prayer for the future plans did not cease.

More snapshots and insights into family life

The 'usual' life that continued held many unique and special events.

As the children grew up, Omar loved to spend time with them individually. He took his daughters out on Daddy-daughter dates, plied them with thought-provoking questions and spent time listening as they shared their hearts. Rachel fondly remembers her dad ordering her first knickerbocker glory. Those moments were precious: a time of connecting about silly things when she was young but later becoming times of deep discussions. These were often spiritual or about plans for the future, and were always full of faith and hope. There were also plenty of embarrassing moments, such as Omar intently asking the waitress, 'What would you recommend?', 'How long have you been working here?' and announcing, 'This is my daughter – she's getting married soon!' Rachel reports that, 'Above all, the times were full to the brim with encouragement, like no other. He would say how proud he was of me, how special I was, that the Lord had plans for me, and he encouraged me to use my gifts. He would voluntarily share his desires and heart with me, and would relay his five-year plans, his hopes, his dreams.'

Sarah remembers feeling exceptionally spoilt on these dates and how Omar always showed concern about how she was and about her walk with God. She never felt judged by him; even if he did not agree with everything she did, he never made her feel bad. She also remembers many random acts of kindness, such as when her hair straighteners broke; knowing how important they were to her, Omar drove her straight to Argos to choose some new ones. When Sarah lost her phone, Omar had no qualms about buying her a replacement. Another time, when she mentioned needing an external hard drive, Omar disappeared out to the shop and was there and back before anyone had even realised he had left the house! Sarah also recollects how Omar always made her feel special and as a teenager whenever she got ready to go out, he would tell her how beautiful she looked.

With Tim, Omar competitively played snooker at home on his small snooker table. This was serious business and Omar would not be at all pleased if his ten-year-old son came close to winning. Being high-spirited, shouts of joy could be heard all over the house and probably outside, too, whenever Omar potted a ball. Omar and Tim also spent time watching football at home, especially if their team, West Ham United, was playing. And at least once each football season they would go to watch a home match. In later years, they would go to the local café or pub where they would talk about Tim's hopes and plans for the future and discuss his interest in finance.

There was never any doubt about how much Omar loved his children and how special they were to him – he must have told them practically every day. The same went for his wife, Gill, who was once informed by a work colleague of his that she had surmised by discussions with Omar that he was besotted with Gill.

Omar loved to entertain and people were always welcomed into the family home. The Ganie children grew up in a very sociable environment and enjoyed befriending and being befriended by the many guests. Whenever friends were invited for a meal or any other occasion, Omar could be observed pacing the room animatedly, awaiting their arrival. He frequently looked out of the window, lifting the net curtain and announcing loudly, 'They're here', or suggesting he ring them if they were more than five minutes late.

For a number of years, Omar and Gill also enjoyed welcoming church friends into their home weekly or bi-weekly for home group meetings where they sang worship songs, prayed and studied the Bible together. At the end of such evenings, Omar would encourage the group to hold hands in a circle and look each other in the eye and say the Grace: 'May the grace of the Lord Jesus Christ, and the love of God, and the fellowship of the Holy Spirit be with you all, evermore, Amen,' found in 2 Corinthians 13:14 in the Bible.

Over the years, an extensive library of Christian books and Bible commentaries developed. These were accumulated by Omar raising additional funds by doing extra marking for external exam boards. He then enjoyed choosing and ordering his books from The Christian Book Distributers in America and would excitedly await their arrival. He loved to search the Scriptures and with the help of these commentaries was able to achieve some in-depth study. He could often be seen sitting next to a huge pile of books, scrutinising their contents and avidly making notes.

To teach or preach from the Bible was one of Omar's heart's desires and he particularly had a heart to teach prophetically (see Appendix). He was often led by God to share encouraging words relating scripture to current situations. He had opportunities to preach at his local churches, particularly at Canning Town Elim Church and Little Ilford Baptist Church, where he also ran a small Bible school with his friend Bill, for those keen to go deeper into the word of God. For a number of years, he was a member of the Baptist preaching circuit, which gave him many opportunities to preach. Also, Omar often taught at a discipleship course called 'Kingdom Keys', which was run by a friend of his. He additionally had a desire to encourage men and organised many men's meetings. He was keen to help motivate men to reach their full potential and to use the gifts that God had given them.

Perhaps it was the 'teacher' in him that rendered it essential to take a notebook to any and every meeting he attended. You would never see Omar in church without his Bible, notebook and pencil; it was not just any pencil – it had to be an ultra-thin lead, revolving type pencil! He always ensured he had a supply of these special pencils readily available. Omar was also renowned for *always* taking Polos wherever he went. He frequently produced them and offered them around to all and sundry!

Omar's generous nature revealed itself in a number of ways, such as whenever he took anyone out for a meal he would ensure they felt comfortable enough to choose anything on the menu by deliberately choosing the most expensive meal himself, thus giving them licence to do likewise. His generosity did backfire once when he felt God prompt him to take a couple supermarket shopping and told them to fill their trolley. This they did – and had Omar trembling in his boots when the bill came to £600 at the checkout! Another time, knowing it probably would not be returned, he practically promised all of his and Gill's savings as a loan to a friend...before Gill stepped in and dissuaded him on the wisdom of this.

In worship to Jesus, Omar was equally extravagant. He would worship at home, pacing up and down in the living room, arms in the air, singing to the Lord. His children all remember hearing him shouting out in prayer in the mornings – it became a frequent wake-up call. He would also have many times of reflective prayer, including intercession for his family, and could often be found on his knees, crying out to God. Likewise, he encouraged family prayer times, being keen to lead the family in God's ways and encouraging them to trust Jesus in all situations.

Once, when singing away with a CD playing in the car – getting fully carried away as usual – Omar stopped at traffic lights and a car pulled alongside him. The driver said, 'I don't know what you're on, but I want some of that!' 'JESUS!' came the animated reply from Omar.

Although Omar was not *always* noisy, it was generally very evident that he was present in the house – especially on the stairs. There was probably no one who could outdo his impression of a stampede of elephants when climbing or descending the stairs! Bath time was an equally noisy affair, with much sploshing, splashing and 'oohs' and 'ahs' – much like a baby whale having a bath! There was usually a running commentary on most events – even minor ones, such as a mislaid watch, which was a common occurrence. Omar would race around the house hunting, stating repeatedly, 'I've lost my watch; has anyone seen my watch?' The family usually took little notice, although Omar appeared to believe there was a major hunt going on for said lost item. Then after five or ten minutes he would find it, wave it in the air triumphantly and announce loudly, 'It's OK, I've found it', to which came little or no response from his family, who were accustomed to these antics. To his credit, Omar was amazing at finding things and if anyone else in the family lost or mislaid anything, he would be the first to down tools and start hunting.

Being a busy man and usually in a rush, even if there was not a time frame to be kept to, there was usually one in his head: the clock was always ticking! Omar's driving was one reflection of this aspect of his personality, much to his family's despair. He was very much a fast-lane driver, loving to weave in and out to reach his destination in the shortest time possible – like a boy racer, in his Renault Megane Scenic family car! He had a special way of changing into fifth gear as though he was so pleased to reach the fifth-gear speed: a little look of determination would appear on his face, he would purse his lips and then lean forward slightly and with an exaggerated movement, place the gear stick into its rightful place. Then there would be a little satisfied smile as if he was the only one on the road to have achieved such a feat! Parking was quite a mission, with much groaning and heaving on the steering wheel, and facial expressions as if parking a juggernaut rather than a car with power steering! Or he would simply jump out and ask his wife to park, as he recognised that she was far more skilled in this area.

Gardening was similar. Omar loved to prune: he was once happily pruning the honeysuckle and as Gill looked out of the window, she could see he was getting dangerously close to the clothesline. As she started to say, 'Be careful you don't…ohh!', Omar looked up and said, 'Oh shucks, babes, I've cut the clothesline!' Another time, they were pruning the garden together and Gill, being more conservative, just wanted the plants cut back a little. They had taken years to reach the height of the fence, which had been her aim. As Gill needed to pop out, she left Omar to it which, on reflection, may not have been the best idea. Upon her return an hour or so later – shock – all the plants had been pruned just about as low as they could go! In the middle of the garden was a mountain of cuttings and Omar standing, looking very satisfied with his work. Gill was dismayed and shook her head in disbelief but was reassured that it was for the best and they would grow back stronger. This proved, in fact, to be true – and became an important illustration to the family over the next few years when facing a number of challenges.

John 15:1-4 says: *'I am the true vine, and my Father is the gardener. He cuts off every branch in me that bears no fruit, while every branch that does bear fruit He prunes so that it will be even more fruitful. You are already clean because of the word I have spoken to you. Remain in me, as I also remain in you. No branch can bear fruit by itself; it must remain in the vine. Neither can you bear fruit unless you remain in me.'*

Omar loved to talk and always had an available (sometimes reluctant) listener in Gill, and he regularly talked at length, sharing his hopes and dreams. She would be entertained with new discoveries that he had found in the Bible or interesting newspaper articles and even events that took place on the short walk to the newsagent and back. Whilst he chatted away, Gill sometimes drifted into her own thoughts then returned to catch the gist of 'Thought of The Day with Omar Ganie'. He would also listen to Gill, who enjoyed telling in-depth accounts of certain events; however, he would often be on the edge of his seat suggesting she get to the point as if saying, 'Leave out the detail, just tell me the end of the story!'

Being well read and having an excellent way with words, Omar was the one the whole family relied on to assist with CV writing, job applications and suchlike. No one needed a thesaurus when they had Omar! When Gill pursued a degree in public health nursing, he proofread every single assignment that she wrote and helped make changes to the grammar.

Over the years, Gill got used to daily weather updates: how today's weather compared to this day, ten, twenty or so years ago or how this was the hottest, wettest, windiest day ever on record. She also received weather reports from various other countries of interest, especially South

Africa and India. In addition to this, there were regular reports regarding the Sterling versus the South African Rand exchange rate – even a prophesy that the Rand would weaken to 20 Rand to the pound by 2015, which turned out to be correct!

Chapter 8

Vocation

'Jesus said, "I am the way, and the truth, and the life. No one comes to the Father except through me."'
John 14:6

Omar was not a man to shy away from controversy; being a person of strong views, ethics and morals it was generally important that these views should be shared! Friends and family were regularly caught up with his audacious ventures, particularly the time Omar wrote to the local newspaper opinion page in reply to an Imam who had proposed that certain schools in the borough of Newham should be made Muslim-only schools. Omar believed this to be exclusive and divisive, and with England being a 'Christian' country, should not be tolerated. He wrote a letter and within it quoted from John 14:6 in the Bible: 'I am the way and the truth and the life. No one comes to the Father except through me.'

As he dropped the letter into the post box, he did what he believed was right, whilst having feelings of trepidation as to what the outcome would be. Indeed, the blue touch paper was well and truly lit: within two weeks of the letter being published, there were demonstrations by pupils displaying placards at his school stating 'Ganie out', local media coverage, calls for Omar's resignation and appeals that he make a public apology. The story ran for fifteen weeks in the local newspaper, with many views on either side. At one point, the head teacher advised that he take some time off work but throughout this episode Omar did not take one day off; his perseverance in the face of adversity was admirable.

Christians came together to pray and support Omar, although some did question the wisdom of his actions. Omar and Gill received many letters of encouragement during this time, which were much appreciated. Omar's heart was never to antagonise anyone; he loved people and had many friends of different faiths but he was sold out for Jesus, and his prime goal in life was for others to know and love Jesus as he did.

Following his first teaching post in East London, Omar went on to work as Deputy Head of Science at St Edward's Church of England School in Romford, which was rather different from the East End school he had just left. It took time for him to adjust to the middle-class environment – and them to him, with his outspoken ways and constant witty quips. Once he settled in, he made many good friends, especially with his science colleague, Keith Jefferson. Both staff and pupils warmed to this unusual teacher. He spent ten years at this school, becoming Head of Science during that time. The humorous comments on his many leaving cards revealed his popularity and familiarity with both staff and pupils. One pupil commented, 'Mr Ganie – you are so funny, it's not normal!' That was so very true!

Following St Edwards, Omar worked as Head of Science at Bishop Challoner Roman Catholic Girls' School in Tower Hamlets for two years before leaving to spend a year teaching as Head of Science at Central Foundation Boys' School in Islington. Next, he took a slight career change and worked for a year as Boys' Achievement Consultant in Southwark – but he missed the school activity and involvement. He therefore took a post as Head of Science in Archbishop Michael Ramsey School in Southwark. Omar finally settled at Leytonstone Business Enterprise Specialist School in Waltham Forest in January 2004, initially as

Head of Science before being promoted to Assistant Head teacher.

Omar ensured he kept up to date in education and undertook a number of courses including the National Professional Qualification for Headship, Ofsted training and a Master's in Education. In addition to teaching, he worked as an Ofsted inspector between 2009 and 2014, and he prided himself on being fair and personable in this role.[1]

Over the years it seemed that Omar worked harder and longer hours as he strove to achieve the best he could for the pupils he taught, and the staff he supported as Assistant Head Teacher. Most days he worked from 6.30am to 6pm. One of his head teachers commented that Omar was the only teacher she knew who got into work before her – and she thought *she* was dedicated.

Being a man of habit, Omar always prepared his clothes for the following day, all carefully placed on his chair, with particular colour shirts and ties, depending on the day of the week. For example, if it was a green day, then you knew it was Wednesday! In the early years Gill would be up to wave him off as he left for work. As the years passed and he left at the crack of dawn, she would still be sound asleep when he departed. She would often hear him getting

---

[1] (Other courses included: Investing in Diversity for Middle Leaders, Training on Improving Quality of Teaching and Learning, Training on Personalised Learning, Assessment for Learning (AfL) training – EduAction, Improving the Use of Data for all Educators, Embedding AfL Practice in School, Data Management and Target Setting Training, Improving the Quality of Behaviour Management, Developing Global Links – EduAction, Effective Homework Strategies, Data Management in Schools, Improving Quality Assurance of Departments, Improving Literacy in Schools, Curriculum Development in Schools, Developing Leadership and Management in Education and Quality Assurance of Local Education Authorities.)

dressed though, as he hopped about putting his socks on – a task that, apparently, needed to be carried out whilst standing and as quickly as possible!

Whilst at work, Omar would sometimes phone Gill inadvertently while his phone was in his pocket. She would occasionally listen in to his day for maybe ten minutes and was usually astounded by what he accomplished in that time. He once popped into a history class and was asked to cover for a few minutes, with a textbook placed in his hand. Gill heard him saying, 'Right, OK, um, Henry the Sixth – who can tell me about him?' He was totally out of his own subject area. Gill could almost hear the brain cogs going around as he quickly read and hopefully offered some useful information. The class teacher returned and, phew!, he was off – greeting people as he walked down the corridor, reprimanding pupils as he went: 'Why are you here? Where should you be? Stop chewing. What *are* you wearing on your feet? You should be in class!'etc.

Being an Ofsted inspector proved invaluable to the school when they underwent an inspection, as Omar was able to give constructive support during this time. The usual procedure that Ofsted followed would be to give a school only a few days' notice of their pending arrival. Omar's friend and colleague, Head of Science, Atif, recalls that when Omar discovered Ofsted were due to come, he went to find Atif with great urgency. He tracked him down in the men's toilet, where he duly commenced hammering on the toilet door announcing, 'Atif, Atif, Ofsted are coming!' 'What – now?' Atif responded. 'No next Monday,' came the reply; but clearly it was urgent enough to be disturbing Atif at this precise moment!

Omar and Atif became great friends over the years. Atif was a devout Muslim and Omar, being a devout Christian, had great respect for Atif. They had many lively discussions about their faiths and why each of them considered he was right in his particular beliefs. They were like brothers and loved each other as such; Atif really appreciated Omar's support and guidance in the Science department, especially when he was appointed as Head of Science following Omar's promotion to Assistant Head. They frequently worked on projects in the evening at Atif's house, often instigated by Omar, due to the fact that he loved Atif's mother's delicious curries. Being very much like brothers they would also fall out at times but Omar always attempted to find Atif at the end of the day to ensure they were back on good terms. Sometimes Atif would hide just to wind him up but they always reunited in the end. Following one such occasion, Omar asked Atif for his phone number. 'You've got it,' said Atif. 'I deleted it,' came the reply!

A number of school trips were arranged by the Science department, which always proved to be full of unusual events. On one particular occasion the teachers, including Omar and Atif, took a large group of pupils to Paris. Not having a word of French between them proved this to be a very interesting experience. The first catastrophe occurred upon arriving at the hotel: one of the teachers gave the room keys to all of the pupils without making a note of the whereabouts of each one. Hence the hotel, along with other guests, had pupils distributed throughout with no knowledge of where, exactly, they were. As the 'responsible' adults on the trip, Omar and Atif took it upon themselves to knock on every room door to discover the location of each child. Atif ingeniously decided as he knocked on the doors to announce 'Hello, Mr Ganie here', therefore ensuring if any guests made complaints for being disturbed that Omar would be the one to take the blame! In hindsight, they should have realised that they could have discovered the pupils' allocated rooms from the hotel reception; they would then only have needed to disturb the pupils to discover their individual locations!

With regards to the language barrier, Atif, who was able to use Makaton sign language, decided maybe this would be helpful so when trying to buy some juice, he made the Makaton sign for juice and was pleased to note that this was actually quite effective. Omar, thinking this was some sort of extension of the French language, emulated his friend and was extremely delighted with his newly discovered skill. It seemed a little more effective than his usual ploy of speaking English loudly with a French accent!

Chapter 9

Expanding Family

'All your children will be taught by the Lord, and great will be their peace.' Isaiah 54:13

The first of the Ganie children to wed was Sarah. She was swept off her feet by Adam, a lovely Christian young man from Norfolk. Towards the end of Adam's first visit to the Ganie home, he announced that he had been 'in prayer' for the past two weeks as Sarah had warned him that he would be 'grilled' by her dad! In the Ganies' opinion, Adam was quite posh and there was lots of good-natured ribbing when he would, for example, announce that he thought Sarah looked 'radiant' or when asked if he would like jam on his toast, would reply that that would be 'splendid'. Being a quiet and reflective person, vastly different from Omar, he was frequently disconcerted by Omar's loud, extravagant ways.

When Adam tried to ask Omar for Sarah's hand in marriage, he found it difficult to get a word in edgeways. This resulted in him needing to follow Omar up to his bedroom last thing at night and catch him in a quiet moment before retiring to bed! Adam had a whole speech prepared but he had hardly managed to finish his first sentence when Omar said, 'Yes, of course you can!' Then there were hugs all round before he sent Adam off, happy that he could propose to his beautiful wife-to-be the following day.

The first time that Omar and Adam spent some quality time together, they decided to play 'pitch and putt'. Adam would probably have loved a hole to swallow him up when Omar, in his usual manner, whooped, shouted 'Praise the

Lord, yee-hah!' whenever he managed to hit the ball in vaguely the right direction. Omar noted that the group on the tee behind them were also loudly engaged in their game and he realised only later, when Adam explained, that they were mimicking him! Not that Omar was bothered – as far as he was concerned, *he* was the normal one.

On the morning of Adam and Sarah's wedding everyone was getting ready, Omar putting finishing touches to his speech – all was relatively calm. Then, as Gill was fastening Sarah's bodice, there came an agitated shout from upstairs: 'Babes quick! I need your help; I can't do up my cravat.' Rachel tried to calm him down. 'Dad, Mum's just doing up Sarah's dress!' but still the frantic shouts came. Sarah decided it was best if Mum attended to Dad first! Omar was so proud as he walked his eldest daughter down the aisle to wed the love of her life. Much to Sarah's embarrassment, Omar's speech made her sound like Mother Teresa, but he was speaking honestly about his love for his loving daughter, no holds barred!

There was always a story to relay from Adam's in-law visits. On one occasion, while out on a riverside walk, they came to a lovely quiet, civilised country pub where they thought they would have some lunch. 'Maybe we could eat outside,' Adam suggested tentatively, almost as if he were already anticipating the ensuing commotion. He was given a resounding 'No' by Omar as he crashed through the pub door, unmistakably making his presence felt. As they entered, for some reason Omar and Sarah went to the left of the bar while Gill and Adam headed towards the right. The next thing Adam and Gill heard was a yelp of a dog and Omar exclaiming loudly, 'Oh no, sorry mate I didn't see him there. So sorry. Oh, is he OK? Really sorry, I didn't see him. I didn't mean to stand on him.' Adam and Gill took one look at each other, quickly clocked the toilets and made a hasty retreat. When they reappeared, all was calm; Sarah was somehow oblivious of the hullabaloo and Omar was ready to relay the story of the unfortunate dog.

Omar's youngest and very much Daddy's girl, Rachel, was the next to meet her special man, Mr Matt Fox. Omar was pleased, excited and full of many different emotions – could Matt manage his beautifully spirited (at times) daughter? Just like her brother and sister, Rachel was sold out for Jesus and had a unique boldness that was definitely God-given. Rachel subtly engineered a short meeting the first time her parents met Matt: a five-minute rendezvous at St Pancras train station, where Omar and Gill saw Matt and Rachel off on a journey. Matt, romantically, was travelling all the way to Nottingham with Rachel, where she was attending university, just to help with her bag! As Gill chatted to Rachel, Omar was animatedly talking to Matt, trying to get as much conversation as possible into the limited allocated time. Rachel took regular furtive glances in their direction to check how Matt was holding up. Needless to say, he did well. In fact, it was interesting to note that he and Omar had some similar zany ways. The following year Matt arranged to meet Omar in a café to request Rachel's hand in marriage. Omar, in his usual excitable way, tried to high five the waitress. To his disappointment, she left him hanging!

The wedding day arrived. All preparations of bride, bridesmaids and bride's mum took place in the flat that was to become home for the newlyweds. Rachel looked stunning: dressed and ready for the big occasion. Omar, the proud father, arrived to take her to the church. His friend Atif had given him a lift so as Omar excitedly rushed up the stairs, he bellowed to Atif, 'You can come up Atif!' 'Noo he can't!' Rachel panicked. She did not want Atif to see her before her arrival at the church. Omar took one look at Rachel and announced, 'You look beautiful!' Then he said to Gill, 'Quick babes, take a pic!'

Omar carried the train of Rachel's dress down the stairs, continuing with the compliments whilst helping her into the car. As they approached the church, the nerves were building and when they walked down the aisle, both were very nervous but also full of joy. Rachel vividly remembers Omar's speech – both lovely and embarrassing at the same time! He relayed all her heroic moments; he honoured both her and Matt and then continued by saying how 'people matter'. This was a Ganie family phrase – not one that was said much, but one that was displayed deeply with actions.

Omar had prayed for his children from a very young age regarding who they would marry. He prayed for strong Christian men for his daughters and a gentle yet strong Christian wife for his son. The Lord honoured and answered these prayers and Omar was full of gratitude.

And so, 2012 was Tim's time to get married. He had met and started dating Metna in 2010 and it did not take long for them both to realise they were made for each other. Metna clearly had a gentle and helpful nature and Omar soon informed her that he noticed this quality in her. She also had a quiet strength and it was sweet to observe the influence she had on Tim. He was well and truly smitten. There followed another wonderful wedding, where Metna's dad this time was the proud father walking *his* daughter down the aisle.

The Ganie family get-togethers were loud, raucous occasions. Once the two sons-in-law and daughter-in-law got over the initial shock, they made sure they kept up with Omar's humorous onslaughts. Omar always had so many stories and tales to tell, the world to put right etc.; thus, the only way to be heard at times was to raise the decibel level to talk over him! The family soon got used to talking all at once and family mealtimes were a time when many conversations were taking place, with the various family members dipping in and out of the different conversations. It was great fun, even if a little crazy. Along with this were the numerous high fives, which, as always, were readily produced by Omar.

Being the 'King' of washing up, Omar was always keen for things to be done instantly and would be found promptly in the kitchen at the sink following mealtimes. In fact, before dessert was even served, it seemed imperative that the dishes were washed and he would often announce, 'I'm going to wash de wares' in a West Indian accent like his dad! If you were not quick, there was a risk that your unfinished plate could be whipped from before you in his eagerness to get the job done.

***

Encouraging Promises

On Christmas day 2012 before lunch, as all eight members of the family were gathered, Omar opened his bible and read from the book of Genesis. He became very serious as he shared how he felt like Abraham in the way that God had blessed him. He said he had come to Newham as just one man and within a short space of time, his family had grown and he felt overwhelmed with the blessing of God. It was a special and significant moment; Omar did not take anything for granted – he was full of thankfulness.

When the grandchildren started to arrive, Omar was very excited. Joshua was born first, to Adam and Sarah. Omar would hold him and would repeatedly say, 'Joshua Isaac Mason – Mummy loves you, Daddy loves you, Granddad loves you, Nana loves you and Jesus loves you!' Next, baby Gracie was born to Matt and Rachel – there were more excitable times and a granddaughter to love. Omar was about the happiest ever granddaddy!

Over the years, Omar spoke prophetically** (one of the spiritual gifts in the Bible) into many people's lives. He had quite an unusual boldness and if he believed God was saying something, even if it made little sense to him, he would still share it. Two weeks after joining Tower Hamlets Community Church in 2012, Omar received a prophetic word to encourage the church and asked the pastor, Tony Uddin, if he could share it. He shared 'Winter is Over and Springtime is Here', based on verses from Song of Solomon. It was a very significant word for the church at that time and many were encouraged.

> *See! The winter is past; the rains are over and gone. Flowers appear on the earth; the season of singing has come, the cooing of doves is heard in our land. The fig tree forms its early fruit; the blossoming vines spread their fragrance. Arise, come, my darling; my beautiful one, come with me." Song of Solomon 2:11-13.*

On another occasion, while praying with his daughter Sarah and her husband Adam one day in 2012, Omar had a 'picture' of Sarah standing outside a new-build house which he felt she and Adam would own. She had a child on her hip and one standing by her side, and she was full of joy. Omar said that this time next year she would have a son. They were living in a small, rented property at the time with no idea how a house purchase would be possible! God brought this picture to reality: the following year, Joshua was born. Then at the beginning of 2016, the family miraculously bought and moved into a new build, three-bedroom house, and a few months after that Noah Omar was born. God proved himself to be faithful time and time again.

**1 Corinthians 12:1-11*

*Now about the **gifts of the Spirit**, brothers and sisters, I do not want you to be uninformed. You know that when you were pagans, somehow or other you were influenced and led astray to mute idols. Therefore I want you to know that no one who is speaking by the Spirit of God says, "Jesus be cursed," and no one can say, "Jesus is Lord," except by the Holy Spirit.*

There are different kinds of gifts, but the same Spirit distributes them. There are different kinds of service, but the same Lord. There are different kinds of working, but in all of them and in everyone it is the same God at work.

*Now to each one the manifestation of the Spirit is given for the common good. To one there is given through the Spirit a message of wisdom, to another a message of knowledge by means of the same Spirit, to another faith by the same Spirit, to another gifts of healing by that one Spirit, to another miraculous powers, to another **prophecy**, to another distinguishing between spirits, to another speaking in different kinds of tongues, and to still another the interpretation of tongues. All these are the work of one and the same Spirit, and he distributes them to each one, just as he determines (emphasis added).*

Romans 12:3-8

*For by the grace given me I say to every one of you: Do not think of yourself more highly than you ought, but rather think of yourself with sober judgment, in accordance with the faith God has distributed to each of you. For just as each of us has one body with many members, and these members do not all have the same function, so in Christ we, though many, form one body, and each member belongs to all the others. We have different gifts, according to the grace given to each of us. If your gift is **prophesying**, then prophesy in accordance with your faith; if it is serving, then serve; if it is teaching, then teach; if it is to encourage, then give encouragement; if it is giving, then give generously; if it is to lead, do it diligently; if it is to show mercy, do it cheerfully (emphasis added).*

Omar - 4 years old

Omar - 12 years old

In Boys Brigade uniform

Graduation photo

Omar and Gill Wedding

Clockwise from bottom left: Omar, Joe (brother-n-law), Gill (Omar's wife), Ana (sister), Radha (mum)

Omar and Gill's 30th wedding anniversary

The growing family - left to right: Rachel, Gracie, Matt, Omar, Gill, Sarah, Tim, Metna, Adam, Joshua

Chapter 10

Not an Accidental Birth

'For you created my inmost being; you knit me together in my mother's womb. I praise you because I am fearfully and wonderfully made; your works are wonderful, I know that full well.' Psalm 139:13-14

One day in January 2007, whilst sorting through some papers, Omar inadvertently mislaid his British birth certificate. He was really quite distraught, especially as this was the unusual birth certificate divulging that he was born in South Africa then registered in the UK two years later. Omar feverishly trawled through the litter in the large green wheelie bin at the front of the family home in East London. However, it was to no avail; the certificate was gone for good. To try to replace this precious piece of history he needed to apply to the General Register Office (GRO) based in Southport, Lancashire.

It was not too long before Omar was stunned to receive a phone call from the GRO asking him a quite shocking and disturbing question. 'Mr Ganie, do you realise that you have an adoption certificate?' How could this be? He was forty-nine years old; how could the discovery that he might be adopted possibly be true? Immediately, he phoned his mother who adamantly denied that he was adopted and assured him that she and his dad were both his birth parents. It was very confusing! Who to believe? The authorities or his mum? Something was not right, but who was telling the truth? And what about the two-year gap between his birth and being registered? Omar's parents were now divorced and had been so for almost thirty years.

Later that summer Omar received a copy of his British birth certificate but it was nothing like the original one that had been lost. The nearest copy to the original was an old black and white one, which was heavily embossed in black. But where could evidence of his original birth documents be found? On questioning his mother Radha, she informed him that his dad had taken all of his personal documents to court to register him. Omar, as determined as ever, kept asking her if she had any evidence about his birth or anything that told him about his life before the age of two. Radha became upset by all the investigative questioning and kept reiterating that his dad had taken care of everything.

It was important for Omar to discover more about his origin and his history, but his main motivation was to be able to prove that he was born in South Africa and therefore apply for South African Citizenship. He believed he was truly going 'home' to South Africa to serve God there. Over the next few years, Omar searched, questioned and spent much time trying to hunt down evidence about his birth. The more he discovered, the more mysterious it all became. Later that year when he went to The Western Cape Archives and Records Services in Cape Town, South Africa, he was told he needed more information about the hospital where he was born and also needed permission from Home Affairs. His mother always reported that she could not remember where he was born and stated that it was a traumatic time and her brothers had organised everything.

Through more investigating and by meeting with a social worker from Newham's Adoption Support Team, an application was made to court for Omar's birth records. Finally, in 2010, Omar had another meeting with the social worker who was able to give him more information. Apparently, he had been named Goolam Mohamed Akoom initially, had then been adopted by his father, Ray Ganie, and had his name changed to Omar Ganie in February 1960. Omar's birth father's name was not given by his mother at the time of the adoption application. On the paperwork it stated that Omar's father was a Muslim based in Pietermaritzburg and that he disappeared when Radha became pregnant. Radha reported to the authorities that she had left her son in the care of family and returned to collect him after her marriage.

So much did not seem to add up. Upon gaining this new information, Omar again questioned his mother, asking for reassurance as to whether his dad, Ray Ganie, was actually his birth father. His mother insisted that he was Omar's dad – though she could not fill in the missing gaps. She told Omar that she left him in South Africa for just a few months before fetching him. She said it was due to the time lapse between his birth and registering him that Ray was required to adopt him, even though he was actually his birth father. What could Omar do but believe this to be true? During his years growing up, nothing had ever been said that would suggest otherwise. Around this time, he also rang his dad and asked him about the circumstances surrounding his birth. This time it was a different story. His dad bluntly said, 'I'm not your dad!' Omar was stunned and hurt but did not actually believe what he heard; he thought his dad was simply being vindictive. Sadly, that was the last time they ever spoke.

Omar now needed to gather together all his documents, including his parents' marriage certificate, his mother's birth certificate, the copy of his original birth certificate and his current birth certificate and paperwork, to link them together in order to prove that Goolam and Omar were in fact the same person. He understood that his name had been changed but continued to believe that his mother was telling the truth regarding his parentage. Over the next few years, these were presented to a number of authorities in South Africa, usually causing the same perplexed reaction. Copies were taken and then Omar would wait for an outcome – usually nothing! There were comments like, 'We need your father's birth certificate, you need to prove your father is South African', 'We've lost the documents', 'The printer's not working', etc.

Then, finally, breakthrough came in 2011: Omar came across an organisation called Immigration Consulting South Africa (IMCOSA). He contacted them and found that they were based in Roeland Street in Cape Town; he sent all the required documents to them. Nonetheless, many more emails ensued and there were even requests for yet more documents. What relief and joy when, at last, in September 2012, Omar was granted South African Citizenship!

Chapter 11

Grace and Truth

'Fear not, for I have redeemed you; I have called you by name, you are mine.' *Isaiah 43:1*

Omar sounded overwhelmed, excited, even a little confused, as he rang his wife Gill from work on this particular day in 2012. She was busy at her workplace and wondered what the urgency was; although, knowing her husband well, there was often a story to tell, some exciting news to relay or suchlike. Today was no different, although slightly more mind-blowing. 'Babes…my dad *can't* be my dad – I've just seen the shipping logs!' Omar went on to explain how, in his search for the truth surrounding his birth, he had found shipping logs online from 1954 when his 'dad' had arrived in the UK from the West Indies and also from 1959 when his mum had arrived in the UK for the first time from Cape Town, South Africa. His 'dad' had never travelled to Cape Town, or, in fact, anywhere else in the world! Omar was born in May 1958, so it just did not add up.

Feeling somewhat overwhelmed and confused by this discovery, Omar sought out his good friend at work, Atif, who was able to console and support him. He then felt strengthened and encouraged, and able again to pursue his history despite the knowledge that he may not ever truly discover the truth about his actual birth father.

Although all the events surrounding Omar's birth may never be known, it must certainly have been very traumatic for his mother Radha.

So, what was the actual story?

Following the discovery of the shipping logs Omar decided he needed once more to confront his mother. Together with Gill, he visited his mum and as they were chatting, he mentioned Somerset Hospital in Cape Town. His mum immediately said, 'That's where you were born', as though it had suddenly come to her mind. Omar was pleased that, after trying to discover this for so long, at last he knew the exact place of his birth. He then broached the subject of who his dad might be. Initially, his mum was adamant that Ray Ganie was his father but she could see that Omar would not believe this in light of the new evidence. She waited until Omar went out of the room and confided in Gill that there had been another man in Pietermaritzburg, South Africa, with whom she was in a relationship before she met Ray. When she became pregnant, she knew it would be a big family scandal and also that her father would insist on the baby being placed in an orphanage.

When Omar returned to the room Radha said that to protect him, her unborn baby, she went to Cape Town, gave birth there and left him in the care of family friends. She then went to England, met her pen friend Ray Ganie, fell in love and married him. She then returned for Omar – called Goolam Mohammed Akoom at that time – nearly two years later, by which time she was expecting his sister Ana. She said that the Akoom couple, with whom she had left Omar, had wanted to adopt him as they had no children of their own. Therefore, when she arrived to retrieve him, they did not want to release him. Radha said she informed them that she wanted to take Omar shopping; instead, she quickly took him and boarded the ship back to the UK. This must have been very traumatic for all involved and most of all for this innocent child, who by then would not have recognised his own mother.

Imagine the situation: Radha, a beautiful Hindu woman, was unmarried at the age of thirty-one. There is mystery surrounding her apparent relationship with a young man who lived nearby, possibly kept secret due to their different religious backgrounds – this love was never to be, as he was a Muslim. When Radha discovered she was pregnant it seems this man, to whom she had given her heart, no longer wanted to be involved in her life. She confided in her brother and together they agreed that she needed to move away quickly and give birth in another part of South Africa – in Cape Town.

And so this well-kept secret was out – all those years of raising Omar with never a suggestion that Ray was not his birth father! Radha made Omar promise that he would not tell his sister Ana; it seemed that his parents had made a pact to never disclose this information to their children.

Omar felt very much that, like Moses, he was hidden to be kept safe. If he had not been hidden and then retrieved, his life would have turned out remarkably differently. He may have been raised in the orphanage, possibly adopted, and undoubtedly would have experienced a very different cultural and religious upbringing. Omar, knowing from a young age that his ultimate destiny was eternity in Heaven with Jesus, was always thankful to God for His protection and provision.

One fact that his mother had told Omar several times was that when she was in Cape Town at a gathering around the time of his birth, a man came up behind her and said, 'Everything is going to be all right.' He then disappeared out of sight, and it was her feeling that he was an angel. So God's hand was there right from the beginning, weaving a golden thread through Omar's life, keeping him safe, directing his life in ways that at times were hard to understand. But God was graciously guiding him to the knowledge of Jesus as his Lord and Saviour, which was to affect both his and his family's lives for eternity. There were many circumstances in Omar's life about which he knew nothing until the age of forty-nine years. Even then, many more remained a mystery but one thing was for certain: God foresaw, foreknew and fore-loved this very special man who, in spite of many difficult circumstances, grew to be a loving, much loved, crazy, zany, beautiful person.

Chapter 12

South Africa: The Calling

'Show me your ways, Lord, teach me your paths. Guide me in your truth and teach me, for you are God my Saviour, and my hope is in you all day long.' Psalm 25:4-5

Many years had gone into praying to God for clear direction in Omar and Gill's lives. They sought to serve Him wholeheartedly in all that they did. They strongly felt God had work for them to do in South Africa and believed now was the time to start exploring this calling. It was March 2007 and the decision was made to book flights for July that year, to go to Cape Town for three weeks. Sitting at the computer together and not knowing where they would stay or with which church they would link, the flights were booked. The following Sunday at church, a lady called Daphne, from Cape Town, was sitting directly in front of Omar and Gill. Gill took the opportunity to discuss with her the forthcoming trip and enquired about Daphne's home church. Immediately, with no introduction, Daphne's friend Claudine turned around and announced that she and her husband Victor had a house in Mitchells Plain, Cape Town, and that Omar and Gill were more than welcome to stay in it and attend her church. She said her pastor would pick them up from the airport; it was all practically arranged there and then!

Everything just came together. Omar got in touch with the education offices in Mowbray and arranged school visits; Gill connected with The Red Cross Children's Hospital and with several orphanages; and with Claudine's help they linked up with Roger, the pastor at Cape Town Christian

Fellowship, which was the local church in Bridgetown, on the Cape Flats.

Upon their arrival to Cape Town and to the church, they were bowled over by the welcome they received; Omar, especially, felt that he had come home. So many new friendships were made on this first visit, especially with Angus and Kathy who were to become firm friends. Among many others, a close connection made was with a lady called Venice, who made the most amazing fish curry about which Omar would constantly rave!

Over the next seven years, Omar and Gill accomplished eight of these trips. They never ceased to be amazed at the ways God opened doors to give them opportunities to serve Him. For the first two years they stayed in Victor and Claudine's home; then, following Victor and Claudine's return to Cape Town, they found alternative convenient accommodation in Rondebosch. From the first visit, the pace was constant. In addition to Omar's work in education and Gill's support in a local orphanage, they attended church home groups and prayed together with many people from the local church, where Omar was also invited to preach. Both Omar and Gill felt that it was a time of great blessing.

Each year, Omar's work in South Africa increased. He served by carrying out training sessions in schools and also by arranging training sessions out of school hours. From 2008, he formed links with the Director of Quality Assurance at the Western Cape Education Department and for seven years consecutive years, whilst in Cape Town, he provided training for the Quality Assurance Team. He also visited many schools to give support and advice and to try to encourage teachers, who often felt demoralised in their difficult work environment.

Other training opportunities that Omar organised involved training school management specialists and providing training for a National Education Evaluation and Development Unit team on inspection procedures. He also trained principals and school leaders in relation to raising achievement, carried out training for the National Professional Teachers Organisation of South Africa, and trained school educators regarding Assessment for Learning.

Omar was passionate about helping to improve the landscape of education in South Africa; his heart's desire was to see these young students aim high and achieve more than they ever dreamed possible. He also helped to establish protocols and a framework for learning walks to be part of Whole School Evaluation. All the knowledge that Omar gained in the UK, he was keen to share in South Africa to help facilitate learning. In addition, he collected many resources from the UK to be used in schools and in the education offices of Cape Town.

In 2008, whilst in Cape Town, Omar and Gill took the opportunity to visit Durban and Pietermaritzburg, as Omar was keen to explore his mother's and grandparents' homeland and also to meet some family members. It was a fascinating visit – they found the house where his mother had been raised. They also found the area where his grandfather had worked and even the orphanage, of which his grandfather had been one of the founders. This is where Omar would have been placed if his grandfather had been given the opportunity. Whilst in Durban they also spent time with some of Omar's cousins, whom he had not seen since he was a child.

***

It became a regular custom for Omar and Gill to go up on Table Mountain in Cape Town each year; Omar would read Isaiah 40 aloud just as he had initially, when the whole family were there in 1999.

Comfort, comfort my people, says your God. Speak tenderly to Jerusalem, and proclaim to her that her hard service has been completed, that her sin has been paid for, that she has received from the LORD's hand double for all her sins.

A voice of one calling: "In the wilderness prepare the way for the LORD; make straight in the desert a highway for our God. Every valley shall be raised up, every mountain and hill made low; the rough ground shall become level, the rugged places a plain. And the glory of the LORD will be revealed, and all people will see it together. For the mouth of the LORD has spoken."

A voice says, "Cry out." And I said, "What shall I cry?" "All people are like grass, and all their faithfulness is like the flowers of the field. The grass withers and the flowers fall, because the breath of the LORD blows on them. Surely the people are grass. The grass withers and the flowers fall, but the word of our God endures forever."

You who bring good news to Zion, go up on a high mountain. You who bring good news to Jerusalem, lift up your voice with a shout, lift it up, do not be afraid; say to the towns of Judah, "Here is your God!" See, the Sovereign LORD comes with power, and he rules with a mighty arm. See, his reward is with him, and his recompense accompanies him. He tends his flock like a shepherd: He gathers the lambs in his arms and carries them close to his heart; he gently leads those that have young.

Who has measured the waters in the hollow of his hand, or with the breadth of his hand marked off the Heavens? Who has held the dust of the earth in a basket, or weighed the mountains on the scales and the hills in a balance?

Who can fathom the Spirit of the LORD, or instruct the LORD as his counsellor? Whom did the LORD consult to enlighten him, and who taught him the right way? Who was it that taught him knowledge, or showed him the path of understanding? Surely the nations are like a drop in a bucket; they are regarded as dust on the scales; he weighs the islands as though they were fine dust.

Lebanon is not sufficient for altar fires, nor its animals enough for burnt offerings. Before him all the nations are as nothing; they are regarded by him as worthless and less than nothing.

With whom, then, will you compare God? To what image will you liken him? As for an idol, a metalworker casts it, and a goldsmith overlays it with gold and fashions silver chains for it. A person too poor to present such an offering selects wood that will not rot; they look for a skilled worker to set up an idol that will not topple.

Do you not know? Have you not heard? Has it not been told you from the beginning? Have you not understood since the earth was founded? He sits enthroned above the circle of the earth, and its people are like grasshoppers. He stretches out the Heavens like a canopy, and spreads them out like a tent to live in. He brings princes to naught and reduces the rulers of this world to nothing. No sooner are they planted, no sooner are they sown, no sooner do they take root in the ground, than he blows on them and they wither, and a whirlwind sweeps them away like chaff.

> *"To whom will you compare me? Or who is my equal?" says the Holy One. Lift up your eyes and look to the Heavens: Who created all these? He who brings out the starry host one by one and calls forth each of them by name. Because of his great power and mighty strength, not one of them is missing.*
>
> *Why do you complain, Jacob? Why do you say, Israel, "My way is hidden from the LORD; my cause is disregarded by my God"? Do you not know? Have you not heard? The LORD is the everlasting God, the Creator of the ends of the earth. He will not grow tired or weary, and his understanding no one can fathom. He gives strength to the weary and increases the power of the weak. Even youths grow tired and weary, and young men stumble and fall; but those who hope in the LORD will renew their strength. They will soar on wings like eagles; they will run and not grow weary, they will walk and not be faint.*

These were very meaningful verses to Omar and Gill. In 2011 when they took their annual trip to Table Mountain, Omar said he felt Gill should read them and as she did, they both felt the presence of God in a powerful way. Gill was very emotional and knew that this was a significant moment; it was indescribable but there was a feeling that there may not be many more of these moments, so they should hold on to it and stay close to Jesus, who would be there no matter what happened. Omar read the chapter again after Gill and she took some photos as special mementos of that poignant moment.

In 2013, with many friends from Cape Town Christian Fellowship, a celebration meal was held to celebrate Omar's South African Citizenship, which had been granted the previous year. Omar shared his heart about his life and the point to which God had led him so far. He experienced such a strong bond with the people there and felt this was where he belonged. Omar loved South Africa: he felt at home there and truly believed this is where God wanted him to be and to serve Him the remainder of his days.

Chapter 13

Surprising Times

'Delight Yourself in The Lord and He Will Give You the Desires of Your Heart.' Psalm 37:4

Most people who met Omar got a sense that this man wore his heart on his sleeve, and in many ways he expected others to do the same. He was an encourager by nature and the way he would ask, 'How are you?' was done in a way that you knew he meant it. His hand would be on your shoulder, he would look you in the eye and say, 'Yes, but *really* how are you doing?' He frequently told his friends and family that he loved them. Gill was told at least once every day of their marriage that he loved her. During term breaks when he was off work and she was working, he loved to surprise her by cooking a meal, having the table laid with flowers and candles...such a romantic!

Keeping surprises secret was not easy, but one that Omar did manage to keep from Gill was the holiday that he planned for their twenty-fifth wedding anniversary in 2009. He was clearly very excited about it and let a number of other people in on the secret, including their three children – but Gill was left clueless. All she knew was that it was going to cost and she had better work some extra shifts to help fund it!

In between the usual business of life, Omar spent about five years preparing for what was to be a very special holiday. The day arrived and they set off for Heathrow airport, checked in, and waited to board the plane to San Francisco. Omar had bought a camcorder to record the event and it was all very mysterious. As they embarked the flight, Omar secretly handed a note to one of the air hostesses. While they were settling into their seats, the pilot made an announcement on the loudspeaker, saying, 'Congratulations Mr and Mrs Ganie on your silver wedding anniversary. Gill, you may be surprised to hear that you are going to San Francisco, followed by Hawaii, then on to Sidney, Australia before going to Cape Town, South Africa, to renew your wedding vows.' He added, 'Sounds like quite a trip, wouldn't mind doing that myself!' There were many gasps from surrounding passengers followed by Omar handing a very gobsmacked Gill a folder with the itinerary.

Needless to say, it was a holiday of a lifetime, and so beautiful. They met some lovely people to chat to, pray with and share life with, and also had some really precious quality time together. Gill went snorkelling for the first time; they saw manta rays and hammer head sharks, went on a helicopter, visited Pearl Harbour – an amazing time! In Cape Town they were joined by their daughters, Rachel and Sarah, and son-in-law Adam (sadly their son Tim could not make it) and had a wonderful celebration at the church there, where they renewed their wedding vows and shared a meal with their South African friends.

Not many holidays could equal the special anniversary experience but Omar and Gill also enjoyed a wonderful time when they visited India in March 2013. Knowing that this was the place of his ancestral roots made it a particularly significant location for Omar. His mother's family were originally from Andhra Pradesh, Southern India. His great grandparents had moved to South Africa initially to work on a sugar plantation in KwaZulu-Natal. With Omar's new information about his birth father, he realised it was very possible that *his* family also originated from India.

Wow! India was another world – so much for all the senses to absorb! Omar and Gill arrived first in Delhi, where the sheer number of people and vehicles on the streets was unlike anything they had experienced before. There were no road markings to divide the five or six lanes of traffic; there were cars, rickshaws and motorbikes – on which female passengers would ride side-saddle. Cows would also be meandering through the streets, unperturbed by the noise and commotion around them. It was clearly a work of art to safely negotiate these streets!

Omar and Gill travelled by train to Agra, the home of The Taj Mahal, which is an immaculate ivory-white marble mausoleum. It was indeed beautiful but as with Delhi, the surrounding poverty and poor infrastructure were very apparent and were heartrending to observe.

The next destination was Mumbai, a city massively populated and apparently the wealthiest city in India but sadly clearly displaying much poverty; there were many families with young children living on the streets. There were too many people to be able to help them all, but Omar and Gill bought and gave food whenever they went out. It was impossible to walk by so many and do nothing. Omar and Gill also met with a Christian couple whilst there and were inspired that this couple were educating a group of children, and planned to do so up to university level. Many children in India do not have access to formal education and so being able to meet this need, even just for a few, would have had a massive impact on these children's and their families' lives.

Upon leaving Mumbai, there was a strong feeling for Omar and Gill that they would like to return in the future and try to serve the people in some small way. It was a very moving time.

Chapter 14

God's Covenant and Favour

'I have set my rainbow in the clouds, and it will be the sign of the covenant between me and the earth.' Genesis 9:13-15

2014: Omar and Gill always knew this was going to be a significant year – a very special year – but nothing could have prepared them for what lay ahead. Oblivious to the shocking events that were hurtling towards them, they proceeded through life as usual. They were making plans for their future, enjoying the moment and in this, their thirtieth year of marriage, they seemed to be full of joy and growing more in love. Gill would sometimes be left in amazement as she observed the beautiful life with which they had been blessed, and wondered at times if the blissful bubble would ever burst. It was not as if there were not the usual life issues and problems to be dealt with, but it felt as though she and Omar, together with God's help, could face anything.

Life was very busy, with Omar teaching long hours and Gill also working hard and feeling stretched in her Health Visitor's role. As they excitedly prepared to move to South Africa in 2015, they felt sure that this was God's ultimate plan for their lives. It was especially Omar's heart's desire to serve God back in his homeland.

Omar's fifty-sixth birthday was on May 24th and although he and Gill had previously been to Israel for his fiftieth birthday, Omar was keen to travel there again. They arrived in Jerusalem and stayed in a lovely Christian guest house just inside the old city wall… a beautiful city full of biblical history. It is the place where Jesus was crucified and also where he rose from death. There are many verses in the Bible relating to the death and resurrection of Jesus. These are just a few:

Jesus said, 'I am the resurrection and the life. Whoever believes in me, though he die, yet shall he live.' John 11:25

'Now if we died with Christ, we believe that we will also live with him. For we know that since Christ was raised from the dead, he cannot die again; death no longer has mastery over him. The death he died, he died to sin once for all; but the life he lives, he lives to God. In the same way, count yourselves dead to sin but alive to God in Christ Jesus.' Romans 6:8-11

'He was buried, and he was raised from the dead on the third day, just as the Scriptures said.' 1 Corinthians 15:4

Omar and Gill spent the first evening, which was the Sabbath, wandering around old Jerusalem, frequently coming across groups of Jewish men singing and celebrating – a very joyful atmosphere! The week was filled with much exploring and a huge sense of peace and joy, ending with two stunning days in Tel Aviv. It all felt like an oasis, compared with what was a very hectic time back in the UK. Significantly, that year for his birthday gift, Omar's daughter Rachel gave him a CD by The Jesus Culture band called *You Make Me Brave* which he absolutely loved and played continuously for some time. Omar felt a strong desire to buy the same CD for other family members and many friends. Unbeknown to him, a time to be exceptionally brave was indeed coming.

July came, and with it the usual busyness of preparing for the annual trip to Cape Town, South Africa: dates in the dairy, teaching notes to prepare, people to see and, this time, visits to estate agents to start planning ahead for somewhere to live the following year. At the beginning of the two weeks in Cape Town, Omar picked up his ID book from The Department of Home Affairs. He was then able to apply for his passport which, miraculously, was ready within the two weeks that they were in Cape Town. He was also informed that his children would be eligible to apply for South African Citizenship.

Omar met with the Director of Quality Assurance. They discussed work opportunities, from which he surmised that he would be able to gain some paid employment and also serve in a voluntary capacity. Gill's application to the South African Nursing Council was going ahead. Prospects of work looked hopeful and she had a growing interest in undertaking some nursing in rural areas. Excitement was growing and it appeared that God was clearly opening doors.

Together, Omar and Gill visited a township project called The Sozo Foundation, which is a non-profit organisation based in the impoverished Cape Flats community of Vrygrond. This made a massive impact on them. The CEO, Anton, showed them around. There is a gardening scheme: Sozo Eden, a holistic home gardening programme which empowers low-income families to provide nutritious food for their households by developing individual vegetable gardens. There is also the Educentre, which is an after-school tutoring and mentorship programme for high school learners. Additionally, they saw the exciting project of the *new* Educentre which was in the process of being built: this would meet the needs of the students more effectively.

As they stood observing this, a massive rainbow appeared behind it, which they believed was significant; they felt that God was assuring them of his love, faithfulness and covenant. There were clearly aspects of work here in which they could both be involved: Gill in the area of health and wellbeing (another project which was being developed) and Omar with the Educentre. Over the subsequent few days, several more rainbows appeared. Omar repeatedly informed Gill that, 'This is a very significant year – you must not forget this year, this is very significant!' They both journaled the exciting events of this period in Cape Town and felt very humbled regarding how they believed God was going to use them.

> *'I have set my rainbow in the clouds, and it will be the sign of the covenant between me and the earth. Whenever I bring clouds over the earth and the rainbow appears in the clouds, I will remember my covenant between me and you and all living creatures of every kind'. Genesis 9:13-15*

Omar was thrilled to be able to proudly display his South African ID book and passport when preaching at Cape Town Christian Fellowship prior to leaving for home in the UK for the last time before the planned relocation to Cape Town in October 2015. Gill's application for permanent residency was also going ahead. The visit had indeed proved to be very fruitful and one of the most special they had experienced.

Chapter 15

Home Coming

'I have fought the good fight, I have finished the race, I have kept the faith.' 2 Timothy 4:7

Omar and Gill celebrated their thirtieth wedding anniversary on August 25th, 2014. They had a special meal with their children and grandchildren; Joshua had just turned one year old, so it was a double celebration and a very special time, with lots of fun and many photos taken to mark the occasion.

On the same day came the news that Omar's adopted dad had sadly died the previous June. Omar's sister Ana rang to inform him that their mother had just told her this news. (Omar and Ana's mother had dementia and her memory had been triggered by seeing a photo of their father.) Omar had not felt able to contact his dad since being informed by Ray that he was not his birth father. Following this news, during one particular phone call between Omar and Ana, Omar was questioned by Ana regarding their relationship: 'You are my brother aren't you?' Omar knew he must reply with the truth, which was that they were half brother and sister and that he had not been able to tell her previously due to their mother's insistence that he should keep this information secret. He disclosed everything.

A few weeks later, Ana and her husband Joe visited Omar and Gill. Omar was then able to present them with all the information he had collected about his birth and the mystery surrounding it. Ana was pleased that Omar had been able to share this with her. She said if anything, it made her feel closer to him.

The preparations for departing to Cape Town the following year continued in earnest. As part of the preparations, Gill embarked on a diploma in tropical diseases at The London School of Hygiene and Tropical Medicine. This was an intense, six-month course for one day a week, in addition to her usual busy work schedule. Omar was also doing his typical long hours. Consequently, they were both working pretty flat out and felt, at times, as if they were almost running out of steam. A welcome break came in October half term. During this time there was an amazing display of ceramic poppies all around the Tower of London, which commemorated the centenary of the start of the First World War. Omar and Gill went to view this wonderful spectacle and Omar took many photos, including some of Gill, whilst insisting on announcing loudly among the crowds of people, 'I'm just taking pictures of my beautiful wife! Ah look, you look lovely!', much to Gill's embarrassment and onlookers' amusement!

They also had a short trip to Rye in Sussex during this half-term break, where they stayed in a windmill guest house and had fun exploring the town, church, castle and little antique shops. They went into a card shop and Omar noticed a birthday card that read: 'For Our Lovely Granddaughter Aged 2'. He insisted that they should buy it, even though Gracie was not yet one year old! During this time, Omar commented to Gill that his memory did not seem to be very good lately. They both laughed it off as probably being due to stress.

After half term, back at work, it was a difficult term for Omar with lots of extra pressures and stress…

***

Events were about to dramatically change… On Thursday November 6th 2014, Omar collapsed at the end of the school day whilst on duty. He was taken by ambulance to the local hospital and diagnosed with stress and then discharged home. On Saturday November 8th, when Omar woke up, he knew his head did not feel right and he was having difficulty reading. He went with Gill to the Accident and Emergency Department at The Royal London Hospital and received immediate and excellent care. A CT scan was carried out, followed by a more in-depth scan with contrast dye to give a clearer result. Omar was diagnosed with a brain tumour. When he was informed, he calmly looked at Gill and said, 'It's going to be alright; I shall not die but live and proclaim the works of the Lord.' (Psalm 118:17). God's love was surrounding them; it was like being in a bubble of God's grace.

The next four months were filled with faith, courage, treatment, special family times, many quality moments and lots of prayer, safe in the knowledge that God would never leave them or forsake them (Deuteronomy 31:6). Within those four months there was Christmas to prepare for and enjoy. When the day arrived, there was the usual hustle and bustle of the growing family coming together. Plans had been rearranged, to ensure that they were all present this Christmas. They were resolute that nothing would stop them from celebrating this joyous occasion. There was food to prepare, gifts to exchange, toys to share and games to play.

As the camera clicked away throughout the day, it observed much quiet emotion that bubbled beneath the surface: the joy as the children expressed their excitement and the occasional faraway looks of the adults, at times lost in their own thoughts. Gill was making the most of those precious moments, her eyes feeding on the present joy, filing away each memory. Her head was telling her there would be many more Christmases together; her heart was saying something else – yet she felt safe, as if in a bubble. Omar was quieter these days but blissfully happy to be surrounded by his family, which he loved so dearly.

Omar continued to keep remarkably well during the beginning of 2015. There were many answers to prayer and his headaches were minimal. There were lots of memorable times with family and friends. Omar felt very blessed by all the love, support and prayers that he received. He also felt such an amazing presence of Jesus during this time. During the period of treatment and prayer it was not possible to know if the miracle of full health was being restored, although following a week of treatment in mid-March he felt quite unwell. It was a heart-breaking time.

On the 17th March 2015, Omar went to his Heavenly home. The journey continues…

Hebrews 11:1-16

Now faith is confidence in what we hope for and assurance about what we do not see. This is what the ancients were commended for. By faith we understand that the universe was formed at God's command, so that what is seen was not made out of what was visible.

By faith Abel brought God a better offering than Cain did. By faith he was commended as righteous, when God spoke well of his offerings. And by faith Abel still speaks, even though he is dead. By faith Enoch was taken from this life, so that he did not experience death: "He could not be found, because God had taken him away." For before he was taken, he was commended as one who pleased God. And without faith it is impossible to please God, because anyone who comes to him must believe that he exists and that he rewards those who earnestly seek him.

By faith Noah, when warned about things not yet seen, in holy fear built an ark to save his family. By his faith he condemned the world and became heir of the righteousness that is in keeping with faith. By faith Abraham, when called to go to a place he would later receive as his inheritance, obeyed and went, even though he did not know where he was going. By faith he made his home in the Promised Land like a stranger in a foreign country; he lived in tents, as did Isaac and Jacob, who were heirs with him of the same promise. For he was looking forward to the city with foundations, whose architect and builder is God.

And by faith even Sarah, who was past childbearing age, was enabled to bear children because she considered him faithful who had made the promise. And so from this one man, and he as good as dead, came descendants as numerous as the stars in the sky and as countless as the sand on the seashore.

All these people were still living by faith when they died. They did not receive the things promised; they only saw them and welcomed them from a distance, admitting that they were aliens and strangers on earth. People who say such things show that they are looking for a country of their own. If they had been thinking of the country they had left, they would have had opportunity to return. Instead, they were longing for a better country - a Heavenly one. Therefore, God is not ashamed to be called their God, for he has prepared a city for them.

Epilogue

The journey continues for Omar in Heaven. The journey continues for his family and friends here on earth. South Africa is very much on the hearts of the Ganie family and they are keen to continue to support particular projects, especially The Sozo Foundation - thesozofoundation.org.za.

Omar had sent about thirty boxes of educational books and materials to Cape Town in late 2014, in preparation for his and Gill's planned relocation the following year. In January 2016, Gill visited Cape Town with her son Tim and daughter-in-law Metna. They delivered these boxes of resources with the help of friends, Andy and Sue Horne, to various organisations, including The Sozo Foundation Educentre with which Omar had been involved. These were well received and clearly a blessing to the recipients.

Having received his South African Citizenship and then ID book and passport in 2014, Omar was informed that his children would also be able to apply for Citizenship. His son Tim is now also a South African Citizen.

There are many things in life that remain a mystery but one thing is for certain: Jesus has been with us through all the ups and downs. He is our hope for today and bright hope for tomorrow.

Appendix

Teachings by Omar Ganie

Being Prophetic in Your Generation

I believe that being prophetic in your generation involves having a lifestyle that speaks beyond your generation about what God means to you and what He should mean to those around you.

I believe God is looking for a prophetic people in their generation who will:

1. Warn and encourage people about what is to come
2. Point people to Jesus' Second Coming
3. Be watchmen for God's people
4. Declare God's truth
5. Give direction to the church.

Enoch: The First Prophet

Bible References:

Genesis 5: 21-24

When Enoch had lived 65 years, he became the father of Methuselah. After he became the father of Methuselah, Enoch walked faithfully with God 300 years and had other sons and daughters. Altogether, Enoch lived a total of 365 years. Enoch walked faithfully with God; then he was no more, because God took him away.

Hebrews 11:5

By faith Enoch was taken from this life, so that he did not experience death: "He could not be found, because God had taken him away." For before he was taken, he was commended as one who pleased God.

Jude 14-15

Enoch, the seventh from Adam, prophesied about them: "See, the Lord is coming with thousands upon thousands of his holy ones to judge everyone, and to convict all of them of all the ungodly acts they have committed in their ungodliness, and of all the defiant words ungodly sinners have spoken against him."

Points to consider:

- Being prophetic in your generation involves a continuous habitual consistent walk with God. One needs to be purposeful, have direction in one's life and be in regular fellowship with other believers.
- Enoch's name means dedicated; he came to a point in his life at sixty-five years old when he may have reached a crisis – a crossroads experience. Why? We are told that after the birth of his son Methuselah, which means to 'draw out' or 'lengthen', that he walked with God.
- Remember, there was a continual increase in wickedness upon the earth after the sin of Adam and Eve – disobedience, rebellion, giving the enemy ground. Then the sin of murder – Cain/Abel (Genesis 4:8); an increase of wickedness. Genesis 6:1-7.
- Enoch probably could see prophetically what was happening after the birth of his son and named him

'Lengthen the Years Of'. Methuselah did in fact live longer on earth than anyone else; he lived 969 years.

- Methuselah died about the time of the flood. He became the father of Lamech, who became the father of Noah.
- The flood came when Noah was six hundred years old on the seventeenth day of the second month.
- It is clear that Enoch named his son prophetically: 'Draw Out The Years'. God was watching Enoch and was pleased with him, in the same way God is watching over our lives. God is still being merciful to our generation; there is still time for us (the Church) to repent. There is still time for those outside the Church to repent (the world).
- Sometimes crisis causes changes in life and can make one more effective on this earth.

Enoch pleased God so God eventually took him to be with Him – he walked into His presence (Hebrews 11:5)

- The phrase pleased God is related to the walk Enoch had with God.
- Remember: Enoch walked with God in the way described for three-hundred years.
- 'He was no more' means he was not alive on earth; not present.
- Why did God transport him into His presence? Because He wanted him to be with God; Enoch was ready for close, eternal fellowship with God. He was ready to see God face to face. Enoch was not in love with this world; his relationship with God was more important than anything else in his life. Only God mattered to Enoch.

What pleases God?

- Putting Him first – Matthew 22:34-38.

- Loving your neighbour as yourself – Matthew 22:39-40.
- Doing his will (obedience).
- Not sinning.
- Being a servant.
- Having faith in him.
- Developing the fruit of the Holy Spirit.

Proverbs 16:7

When a man's ways are pleasing to the LORD, he makes even his enemies live at peace with him.

John 8:29

The one who sent me is with me; he has not left me alone, for I always do what pleases him.

Romans 8:8

Those controlled by the sinful nature cannot please God.

Romans 15:1-4

We who are strong ought to bear with the failings of the weak and not to please ourselves. Each of us should please our neighbours for their good, to build them up. For even Christ did not please himself but, as it is written: "The insults of those who insult you have fallen on me."

For everything that was written in the past was written to teach us, so that through the endurance taught in the Scriptures and the encouragement they provide, we might have hope.

Galatians1:10

Am I now trying to win the approval of human beings, or of God? Or am I trying to please people? If I were still trying to please people, I would not be a servant of Christ.

Thessalonians 4:1-11

As for other matters, brothers and sisters, we instructed you how to live in order to please God, as in fact you are living.

Now we ask you and urge you in the Lord Jesus to do this more and more. For you know what instructions we gave you by the authority of the Lord Jesus. It is God's will that you should be sanctified: that you should avoid sexual immorality; that each of you should learn to control your own body in a way that is holy and honourable, not in passionate lust like the pagans, who do not know God; and that in this matter no one should wrong or take advantage of a brother or sister.

The Lord will punish all those who commit such sins, as we told you and warned you before. For God did not call us to be impure, but to live a holy life. Therefore, anyone who rejects this instruction does not reject a human being but God, the very God who gives you his Holy Spirit.

Now about your love for one another we do not need to write to you, for you yourselves have been taught by God to love each other. And in fact, you do love all of God's family throughout Macedonia. Yet we urge you, brothers and sisters, to do so more and more, and to make it your ambition to lead a quiet life: you should mind your own business and work with your hands, just as we told you.

Being prophetic in your generation involves speaking about Jesus' Second Coming (Jude 14-15)

- Enoch spoke about these men that they would be judged when Jesus comes again with his angels at the end of the age.

- We need to speak about Jesus' Second Coming in the church and to warn against sinful living.
- Enoch preached about the coming Judgement: God is a God of mercy and judgement.

Noah (meaning 'rest') Genesis 6:1-8

When human beings began to increase in number on the earth and daughters were born to them, the sons of God saw that the daughters of humans were beautiful, and they married any of them they chose. Then the Lord said, "My Spirit will not contend with humans forever, for they are mortal; their days will be a hundred and twenty years."

The Nephilim were on the earth in those days — and also afterward — when the sons of God went to the daughters of humans and had children by them. They were the heroes of old, men of renown.

The Lord saw how great the wickedness of the human race had become on the earth, and that every inclination of the thoughts of the human heart was only evil all the time. The Lord regretted that he had made human beings on the earth, and his heart was deeply troubled. So the Lord said, "I will wipe from the face of the earth the human race I have created — and with them the animals, the birds and the creatures that move along the ground — for I regret that I have made them." But Noah found favour in the eyes of the Lord.

Being prophetic in your generation involves:

- Being righteous.
- Blameless.
- Walking with God:
    - ♦ habitually

- ♦ with direction
- ♦ with fellowship

Noah lived his life in a way that was in complete contrast to the people of his generation, who were extremely wicked in thought and deed. Because of Noah's lifestyle, God spoke to him:

> *'Now the earth was corrupt in God's sight and was full of violence. God saw how corrupt the earth had become, for all the people on earth had corrupted their ways. So God said to Noah, "I am going to put an end to all people, for the earth is filled with violence because of them. I am surely going to destroy both them and the earth.' (Genesis 6:11-13)*

Being prophetic in your generation involves building in the present for the future

- Noah obeyed God and built an ark.
- Noah acted by faith in God – he was in a desert area or an area where it had never rained'.
- It took him one hundred years to build the ark.
- He would have been ridiculed for it but he preached righteousness (2 Peter 2:5).
- The ark represents:
    - ♦ A place of safety and salvation
    - ♦ Deliverance
    - ♦ Redemption
    - ♦ A picture of Jesus, who came to give us life and save us from Death
- As Noah was obedient, he saved mankind – seven people were saved with Noah and animals of every kind.
- God established a New Covenant with Noah and his family, signified by a rainbow.

> *Then Noah built an altar to the Lord and, taking some of all the clean animals and clean birds, he sacrificed burnt offerings on it. The Lord smelled the pleasing aroma and said in his heart: "Never again will I curse the ground because of humans, even though every inclination of the human heart is evil from childhood. And never again will I destroy all living creatures, as I have done. "As long as the earth endures, seedtime and harvest, cold and heat, summer and winter, day and night will never cease." (Genesis 8:20-22)*

> *And God said, "This is the sign of the covenant I am making between me and you and every living creature with you, a covenant for all generations to come: I have set my rainbow in the clouds, and it will be the sign of the covenant between me and the earth. Whenever I bring clouds over the earth and the rainbow appears in the clouds, I will remember my covenant between me and you and all living creatures of every kind. Never again will the waters become a flood to destroy all life. Whenever the rainbow appears in the clouds, I will see it and remember the everlasting covenant between God and all living creatures of every kind on the earth." So God said to Noah, "This is the sign of the covenant I have established between me and all life on the earth." (Genesis 9:12-17)*

When Noah and his family got out of the Ark after the rain had stopped (Genesis 9:1-17), God said to them:

- Be fruitful and multiply.
- Fill the earth.
- Fear and dread of you will fall on all the beasts of the earth, birds, creatures on the ground, fish – all given in to your hands, you can freely eat animals and plants.
- They must not eat meat with blood (living).
- Not to kill humans.

- He would establish covenant with Noah and his sons.
- He would never again destroy the earth by a flood.
- The sign of covenant, the rainbow, will be God's covenant with man and all creation throughout generations. God remembers his covenant; it is an everlasting covenant.

What are you building in your lives, your families and your fellowship? Is your church like an ark – in the present for the future? If you build the right things it will/could save this generation! In Matthew 6:19-21 Jesus said we must store up for ourselves treasures in Heaven, not treasures on earth. What does this mean?

Our Godly actions include:

- Being servants: be faithful in service.
- Loving our enemies and each other.
- Showing the fruit of the spirit.
- Being obedient.
- Being helpful, putting others first.
- Preach Christ everywhere; trust God, live by faith, be prophetic in your generation.

Building A Highway For The Lord - The Garden Of God's Delight

Isaiah 35

The desert and the parched land will be glad; the wilderness will rejoice and blossom. Like the crocus, it will burst into bloom; it will rejoice greatly and shout for joy. The glory of Lebanon will be given to it, the splendour of Carmel and Sharon; they will see the glory of the LORD, the splendour of our God. Strengthen the feeble hands, steady the knees that give way; say to those with fearful hearts, "Be strong, do not fear; your God will come, he will come with vengeance; with divine retribution he will come to save you."

Then will the eyes of the blind be opened and the ears of the deaf unstopped. Then will the lame leap like a deer, and the mute tongue shout for joy. Water will gush forth in the wilderness and streams in the desert. The burning sand will become a pool, the thirsty ground bubbling springs. In the haunts where jackals once lay, grass and reeds and papyrus will grow. And a highway will be there; it will be called the Way of Holiness; it will be for those who walk on that Way. The unclean will not journey on it; wicked fools will not go about on it. No lion will be there, nor any ravenous beast; they will not be found there. But only the redeemed will walk there, and those the LORD has rescued will return. They will enter Zion with singing; everlasting joy will crown their heads. Gladness and joy will overtake them, and sorrow and sighing will flee away.

Relating to the Garden of Eden (Genesis 2):

- What does God want to do with our lives? He wants to turn our wilderness into a garden of delight.
- What produced the garden of God's delight? Mist, flood from above and streams from below.
- What does the garden produce? Spiritual fruit and leaves.
- What maintains the garden? The River of Life, flowing from God's presence (Genesis 2:10).
- Why was the garden a place of God's prosperity? Precious metals and stones (Genesis 2:12).
- Why did God put the perfect man in the garden? God put him in the Garden of Eden to work it and take care of it; he was to have dominion and be a steward for the owner (God) of the garden (Genesis 2:15). Other aspects that were important were rest, safety, worship, obedience and fruitfulness.
- What shall we see when we go to be with the Lord? The Heavenly Jerusalem with walls lined with precious stones, a river flowing from Jerusalem (Heavenly) and trees with fruit and leaves lining the bank (Revelation 22: 1-2).

We will use this chapter (Isaiah 35) to understand what is required to build a highway for the Lord, for the redeemed of the Lord to travel safely.

- The highway for the Lord (verse 8): the point of the prophecy is that God will remove all obstacles and "smooth the way" for His people, enabling them to access the blessings of the Kingdom. Some point the Jews' return from captivity in Babylon and Persia as the fulfilment of this prophecy but the language of Isaiah 35 gives it a broader context, including physical healing and environmental blessings (verses 5–7). The highway of holiness could also be seen to refer to the Way that is Christ (see John 14:6); the way of sovereign grace that redeems us from sin.

- It speaks of when Judah or Israel-Judah are in captivity in Babylon.
- Prophetically, God said that this people would return from captivity and along a highway or road of holiness.
- This would be just like the man-made roads and it would be a road of pilgrimage as people went up to the feasts to meet the Lord in His Holy Temple.

Isaiah 51:3 - God will make her deserts like Eden; Her wastelands like the garden of the Lord. Joy and gladness will be found in her, thanksgiving and the sound of singing. (This has parallels to Isaiah 35:1-2 as they will be captive or are captive in Babylon.)

What does God want to do with our lives?

Before we can be involved actively in building a highway for the Lord, God wants to turn our lives from wilderness (barrenness, void, infertility) to fertility.

- Eden was a picture of fertility; God wanted to make Israel the same.
- Deuteronomy 28:25 – Idolatry and rebellion against God let in Israel's enemies.
- Matthew 24:13 – Stand firm to the end!

Garden of God's delight - Genesis 2:4-25

This is the account of the Heavens and the earth when they were created, when the Lord God made the earth and the Heavens. Now no shrub had yet appeared on the earth and no plant had yet sprung up, for the Lord God had not sent rain on the earth and there was no one to work the ground, but streams came up from the earth and watered the whole surface of the ground. Then the Lord God formed a man from the dust of the ground and breathed into his nostrils the breath of life, and the man became a living being.

Now the Lord God had planted a garden in the east, in Eden; and there he put the man he had formed. The Lord God made all kinds of trees grow out of the ground — trees that were pleasing to the eye and good for food. In the middle of the garden were the Tree of Life and the tree of the knowledge of good and evil. A river watering the garden flowed from Eden; from there it was separated into four headwaters. The name of the first is the Pishon; it winds through the entire land of Havilah, where there is gold. (The gold of that land is good; aromatic resin and onyx are also there.) The name of the second river is the Gihon; it winds through the entire land of Cush. The name of the third river is the Tigris; it runs along the east side of Ashur. And the fourth river is the Euphrates.

The Lord God took the man and put him in the Garden of Eden to work it and take care of it. And the Lord God commanded the man, "You are free to eat from any tree in the garden; but you must not eat from the tree of the knowledge of good and evil, for when you eat from it you will certainly die." The Lord God said, "It is not good for the man to be alone. I will make a helper suitable for him."

Now the Lord God had formed out of the ground all the wild animals and all the birds in the sky. He brought them to the man to see what he would name them; and whatever the man called each living creature, that was its name. So the man gave names to all the livestock, the birds in the sky and all the wild animals. But for Adam no suitable helper was found.

So the Lord God caused the man to fall into a deep sleep; and while he was sleeping, he took one of the man's ribs and then closed up the place with flesh. Then the Lord God made a woman from the rib he had taken out of the man, and he brought her to the man. The man said, "This is now bone of my bones and flesh of my flesh; she shall be called 'woman,' for she was taken out of man." That is why a man leaves his father and mother and is united to his wife, and they become one flesh. Adam and his wife were both naked, and they felt no shame.

- Eden also represents a place of intimacy, fellowship, worship and where God's presence dwelt.
- It was the perfect environment for the perfect man.
- It was the most wonderful part of all the earth.

What was the key to producing this wonderful environment?

Genesis 2:5-6 – The Lord had not sent rain on the earth… but streams or a mist [translated as flood] came up from the earth and watered the whole surface of the ground.

Mist (vapour, flood or stream):

- This can refer to water that came from below the earth and preceded first stages of plant life.
- It could be flood – high flooding of a river.
- Could be a freshwater stream.

Context – Earth was uninhabitable, unproductive in its watery state before special creative care given by YAHWEH!

Remember, just as the mist was like a canopy, we also need total immersion, saturation by the Holy Spirit who comes from above, goes within and then flows from the inside out. (Ref: Matthew 3:13-17: Jesus' baptism in water and Holy Spirit; John 7:37-39: 'Out of your belly will flow rivers of living water.')

To maintain a life that is spiritually fertile we must continue to be (being) filled with the Holy Spirit (Ephesians 5:18).

Living a spirit-filled life

- Eden is a large area and to the east of this area, God created a garden.
- The Lord God made every tree that was beautiful and with edible fruits – an orchard of fruit trees.
- Trees represent character and types of people.

> *Psalm 1:1-6: Blessed is the one who does not walk in step with the wicked or stand in the way that sinners take or sit in the company of mockers, but whose delight is in the law of the Lord, and who meditates on his law day and night. That person is like a tree planted by streams of water, which yields its fruit in season and whose leaf does not wither – whatever they do prospers. Not so the wicked! They are like chaff that the wind blows away. Therefore the wicked will not stand in the judgment, nor sinners in the assembly of the righteous. For the Lord watches over the way of the righteous, but the way of the wicked leads to destruction.*

We have a choice of two lifestyles (see also Deuteronomy 30:11-20).

Blessing is promoted by two kinds of activities:

1. Dissociation from the wicked.
2. Association with God.

It is important to reflect on God's word by/through memory and pondering; this is not just the setting apart of special time for personal devotions – evening or morning – but reflection of God's word in course of daily activity (Joshua 1:8).

> *Jeremiah 17:7-8 – "But blessed is the one who trusts in the Lord, whose confidence is in him. They will be like a tree planted by the water that sends out its roots by the stream. It does not fear when heat comes; its leaves are always green. It has no worries in a year of drought and never fails to bear fruit."*

This tree is not growing wild in the wadis (mud rivers/streams) or planted in fields where amount of rainfall varies but it has been purposely planted by irrigation canals (streams of water) i.e. artificial water channels made for the purpose of irrigation (Proverbs 21:1, Ecclesiastes 2:5-6, Isaiah 30:25).

> *Proverbs 11:20 – The Lord detests those whose hearts are perverse, but he delights in those whose ways are blameless.*

> *Proverbs 15:4 – The soothing tongue is a tree of life, but a perverse tongue crushes the spirit.*

Leaves and fruit

We can be assured that the godly will receive God's blessing and will enjoy life as a free gift.

Regarding fruit:

- It should be seen and pleasing to the eye (Genesis 2:9, Galatians 5:22-24).
- It needs the right environment (hearing the word of God, understanding it and responding to it (Matthew

13:23), and feeding on God's word and being filled with the Holy Spirit).
- Fruit needs to be tasted (Genesis 2:9).
- Fruit needs to be picked/pruned (John 15:1-2).
- Know people by their fruit (Matthew 7:15-20).

Regarding leaves: (Ref: Mark 11:12-14, 20-24 and Matthew 21:18-22)

These can represent spiritual gifts:
- Remember, Jesus looked for fruit on the fig tree.
- He was hungry and somewhere on the road from Bethany to Jerusalem he saw a fig tree in leaf.
- Even though it was not the season for figs, the tree gave the appearance of bearing fruit from the outside.
- Fig trees are in leaf about the same time as fruit – the tree gave the prospect of fruit; it is an unusual tree.
- Jesus used the opportunity to teach a moral lesson and cursed the tree because it made a show of life that promised fruit but was bearing none.
- An important lesson in being fruitful and not being spiritually barren (Jeremiah 24:1-8, Isaiah 5:1-7, Jeremiah 8:13).

What maintains the garden of God's delight continuously? A river flowing from God's presence (Genesis 2:10-14)

Eden represents God's presence, and the river flowed from Eden to the garden. To change a wilderness into a garden you need a constant supply of fresh flowing water. The fresh flowing of the Holy Spirit will also change our environment from wilderness to fruitfulness, beauty and blessing.

Isaiah 41: 17-20 – The poor and needy search for water, but there is none; their tongues are parched with thirst. But I the

> *Lord will answer them; I, the God of Israel, will not forsake them. I will make rivers flow on barren heights, and springs within the valleys. I will turn the desert into pools of water, and the parched ground into springs. I will put in the desert the cedar and the acacia, the myrtle and the olive. I will set junipers in the wasteland, the fir and the cypress together, so that people may see and know, may consider and understand, that the hand of the Lord has done this, that the Holy One of Israel has created it.*

When those who are spiritually poor search for water, the only source will come supernaturally from the Lord God of Israel. He will make many rivers flow, even from the places that are most remote, where it seems impossible.

God causes springs within the valley – God's power to refresh! Canaan was described as a good land of brooks of water, of fountains and springs flowing forth in valleys and hills. God wants to turn your dryness into springs – a release of the Holy Spirit which spouts out with a force (an outpouring that is refreshing to others). Then, supernaturally, God plants in the dry and barren place different types and levels of trees which would naturally not be seen together.

Three Levels:

1. Cedar and Acacia – represent God's presence and power.
    - Cedar – appreciated for durability (coniferous, 40m high), used to build David's house (2 Samuel 5:11); also Solomon's temple (the new temple after exile), which is a figure of stature, grandeur and majesty.
    - Acacia – found in the hot Jordan valley, used for making the Ark and parts of the Tabernacle.
2. Myrtle and Olive trees – represent pleasant smell, purity, prosperity and protection.

- Myrtle – with shining blue/green leaves and fragrant white flowers; the leaves, bark and berries are fragrant – used to make perfume.
- Olive tree – used to make olive oil – used for anointing Kings and Priests (1 Samuel 16:13, 1 Kings 1:39); represents prosperity and unity (Psalm 133).

3. Fir (Pines), Pine (Elm) – both good for shade and Cyprus (Box tree) – type of Cedar: tall, erect.

   All these trees are evergreen: sturdy, tough, hardwood, permanent. Like these trees, people also should be present for those who need shade from the heat of the battle.

As the river flows from God's presence, it splits into four head waters/tributaries. These represent the way that the Holy Spirit desires to work in our lives:

1. Pishon – freely flowing – God wants the Holy Spirit to be freely flowing in our lives.
2. Gihon – bubbler or gusher (from a root, which means to burst forth or draw forth). God's desire is that we should burst forth with the Holy Spirit – hence the release of laughter, tears, shaking etc.
3. Tigris (Hiddekel) – rapid; God's Holy Spirit fell suddenly and was like the mighty rushing wind.
4. Euphrates – bursting, sweet, break forth, or rushing; God's Holy Spirit should be overflowing or flooding out to others in sweet joy.
5. The rivers show the boundaries of Eden – learn to know your boundaries (Galatians 5:25). Let us go forward walking in line, our conduct controlled by the Holy Spirit.

Why is Eden a place of prosperity? Because it contains precious metals and stones. (Genesis 2:12)

- Precious metals and stone are crystalline in nature – perfect regular shapes, made deep inside the earth's crust and at the highest temperatures.
- Precious stones that produce the best crystals are cooled down slowly.
- Gold – speaks of God's presence and His kingship/royalty. Most of the articles in the Tabernacle were overlaid or made of gold. The Ark was covered on the outside and inside with pure gold; gold was used to build the temple and gold was given to Jesus – royalty, preciousness and purity.
- Two precious stones: onyx and bdellium (pearl) – onyx is mentioned in twelve precious stones that covered the breastplate of the High Priest, which was on the ephod (a sleeveless garment worn by Jewish priests). Each stone represented a tribe – four rows, three stones in each row. This was in the way the tribes were arranged around the tabernacle as they camped – there is always a lead tribe or chief of the three (protection). Each stone is different but is in harmony with each other – in the same way church members have different functions but are all part of one body. There is a variation in colour, brilliance and attraction in each stone but they are all precious stones (Psalm 116:15 – Precious in the sight of the Lord is the death of his faithful servants). Each stone had the name of its tribe engraved on it. These are related to:
  - The birth of the tribe (Genesis 29:31-30:24)
  - Father's blessing (Jacob) (Genesis 49)
  - Tribal blessing (Moses) (Deuteronomy 30)
- **Example** - sardius (ruby) is the first stone. It represents Judah and means Odem, which is red. Remember, God puts praise first (psalm 100:4); Judah will take the

common things of life (foal) and link them to choice things (vine). (Genesis 49:8-12)

- **Example** – Onyx, which means to shine with lustre of fire and a flashing forth of splendour. It represents Asher (second-born to Zilpah, Leah's handmaid – see Genesis 35:26); the name signifies blessed or happy, very happy (twenty-seven times). Let him dip his foot in oil (Deuteronomy 33:24-25). This indicates Asher will be a land of olive groves; the pressing out of olives – blessing, prosperity. "May we so dip our feet into the oil of God's Holy Spirit that we may leave behind us that certain imprint which will cause men to say: These have been with Jesus and learned from Him." (Ref: C.W. Sleming)

Of the twelve Tribal stones, it is known that eight are definitely the same as those that are described as the foundations of the New Jerusalem in Revelation 21:19-20. (Ref: https://www.biblestudytools.com/commentaries/revelation/revelation-21/tribal-stones.html#3.21.19.1.)

These stones are particularly unique, as they react when light that is cross-polarised* passes through them; this causes them to exhibit a range of colours that are similar to the colours of the rainbow (the Covenant of Remembering). (Ref: The 12 gems of New Jerusalem, David Pawson https://www.youtube.com/watch?v=L9oFfSJD6ZY.)

*(Cross-polarisation is light that has passed through two filters at 90° to each other).

We need to be like those precious stones and allow God's light to pass through, so that what is inside will be radiated out. Those in Christ will radiate out an image of God. We are not perfect and so will not produce the exact image of God, *that was Jesus* (Colossians 1:15).

Adam's activities in the Garden of Eden – (reflect on the following things)

- Worship and obey – to find rest, be safe.
- This was where he could be in God's presence and have fellowship with Him.
- Work and take care of it – also means to worship and obey; like the priests and Levites looked after the Tabernacle and Temple, etc. *The application for today is that when we are working in the area that God has called us to work (whether secular or within the church), we are doing as God asks. Our area of work will be worship and therefore ministry. We are all called to minister i.e. to serve: to lead the lost world to Christ. We serve as he served. Therefore, our work is very important.*
- God provided a helper – Adam could not find a suitable helper amongst the animals.
- God put him to sleep and did a creative work – He created Eve.
- Woman is made from a part of Adam's side – we are to treat each other with respect and value each other.
- Woman was made for Adam as a helper (partner) so that they could be fruitful and multiply.

Eden will be restored

Revelation 22: 1-5 – Then the angel showed me the river of the water of life, as clear as crystal, flowing from the throne of God and of the Lamb down the middle of the great street of the city. On each side of the river stood the tree of life, bearing twelve crops of fruit, yielding its fruit every month. And the leaves of the tree are for the healing of the nations. No longer will there be any curse. The throne of God and of the Lamb will be in the city, and his servants will serve him. They will see his face, and his name will be on their foreheads. There will be no more night. They will not need the light of a lamp or the light of the sun, for the Lord God will give them light. And they will reign for ever and ever.

BV - #0066 - 180121 - C0 - 203/127/8 - PB - 9781913425180 - Matt Lamination